IN & OUT

1980 Debrett's 1981

IN & OUT

A lighthearted guide to contemporary society
by

Neil Mackwood

PREFACE BY LORD BURGHERSH
DRAWINGS BY LUCY

The views expressed in this work are those of
the author, and are not necessarily shared
by the publisher

DEBRETT'S PEERAGE LIMITED

LONDON   NEW YORK
SYDNEY

To Christo — the world's second greatest snob — who inspired these pages

Text © Neil Mackwood 1980
Illustrations © Lucy 1980
Published by Debrett's Peerage Limited
73/77 Britannia Road, London SW6

ISBN 0 905649 44 3

Printed and bound in Great Britain
at The Pitman Press, Bath

Contents

Preface by Lord Burghersh   ix

Introduction   xiv

1 Snobbery
  The real French dukes   9

2 Schools – To Fag or Not to Fag?
  Boys' prep schools   14
  Boys' public schools   14
  Girls' public schools   15

3 Jobs
  For the boys   19
  For the girls   20
  The Armed Forces – hobby and professional regiments   21
  Models   25
  Interior designers and design   27

4 The Jet Set
  The jet-set year   33
  People you will meet on the way   35

5 The Gossip Column
  How to get IN & how to keep OUT   37
  The cast   43

6 People
  *Dukes, marquesses, earls, viscounts, barons and bearers of
    courtesy titles*   46
  Hostesses   49
  Bachelor and gentlemen hosts   49
  *Girls unlikely to be queen and those still in the
    running*   50
  Ex-kings   50

v

Millionaires 52
Gucci socialists 52
Businessmen who made it – according to The Times 54
Photographers 54
Film directors 55
Mummers 55
Artists 57
The team 57

7 What's in a Name?
Boys 61
Girls 63
Nicknames to drop 64

8 Débutantes – Do They Exist?
Some debs 69
Some delights 69

9 Language
Psycobabble 74
Calspeak 76
Pub talk 76
Media talk: Ripponspeak; gossip buzzwords;
   film/TV/radiospeak 77
Anglo-Jewish 78
Legalese 79

10 Fashion
Tailors 85
Women's shoe shops and designers 86
Men's shoe shops and makers 86
Shirt makers 86
Designers 87

11 The Dinner Party
IN & OUT foods 90
Table furniture 93
Restaurants 94

12 The INs & OUTs of Social Nobility
   So you think you are smart!   100

13 Sex, Manners and Marriage
   Kissing, etc.   104
   INs & OUTs, dos & don'ts   106
   Love tokens – her to him & him to her   108

14 The Garden
   INs & OUTs   113
   Plants   114
   Veg   115
   Fruits   115

15 Sporting Etiquette
   Shooting – dos & don'ts   117
   Fishing – dos & don'ts, rivers to head for   120
   Hunting dos & don'ts, hunts   122
   Yachts and things nautical, clubs, clothes, people, races,
      harbours, dos & don'ts, boats   125
   Skiing, resorts, travel companies, equipment, boots, clothes,
      shops, bindings, ski variations   128

16 Clubs
   Night   135
   Gentlemen's   137

17 Knowledge
   Champagne   138
   Drinks   138
   Chocolates   139
   Scent   140
   Emporiums   140
   Health farms   142
   TV programmes   143
   Cars   143
   Which helicopter? charters   145
   Which plane?   145

Airlines   146
Smokes   146
Dogs – breeds   147
Dogs– names   148
Cats   149
Other pets   149
Holidays, summer and winter   151
Estate agents   152
Fashionable causes and charities   153
Mind improvement, therapy, and growth   153

18 The Music Machine
Papers   155
Groups   155
Record companies   156
Record producers   156
Styles   157
Terminology   157
Radio stations   157
Disc jockeys   158
Pop persons   158
General   158
How IN are you?   159

Preface
LORD BURGHERSH

When Neil Mackwood asked me to write the preface to his second book I was terribly flattered but equally embarrassed. Had he written a first? I certainly had never read it, but that is not saying much since in the nursery I struggled with Enid Blyton and gave up altogether on the second chapter of *Swallows and Amazons* – firmly believing it was a tale about a powerful race of women.

Well, I found out he had when he came to my flat bearing a copy of *In & Out 1979–80*. Ah! I mused – it is a guide to the famous London club in Piccadilly. When he explained it was a social guide I felt like crawling into a corner and dying. Had he noticed that he was drinking second-rate whisky (Scottish nevertheless) from a tumbler which came free with seven gallons of four-star petrol? Had he noticed that I sprawled in the most comfortable chair? What about the shag-carpet or even that my best single malt had been poured for his second drink?

How ghastly! How OUT he must consider me. But if he had noticed he was far too polite to comment. So back to the cheap whisky. And why not? What did it really matter, and what difference was it going to make?

Society today is in a state of flux. First we must ask – does it exist? Of course it does, but how does one identify it? There are 25 dukes, 38 marquesses, 194 earls, 128 viscounts and endless barons – not to mention their countless offspring, legitimate or otherwise, who are alive, well and kicking like mules.

The fact is that when one of these peers' daughters brings home a hairdresser, pop-star or actor (usually at a week-end in the middle of the shooting season) they are appalled. But why? Is this so terrible? Perhaps

ix

They are appalled

these entertainer johnnies want to see how the other 'arf live, or maybe they love the duke's daughter. The duke has nothing much to fear unless his daughter reciprocates the love.

If I may be so bold, there is a bastion of the so-called upper class who are probably members of White's Club, Lloyd's, The Guards Polo Club and the syndicate of Six Mile Bottom – are they really trying to live the life of Riley behind everyone else's backs?

Almost without exception the nobility of today have been forced to seek employment of some kind. Gone are the days when it was considered bad form to take a job if you did not need the money, thereby depriving some less fortunate person of a chance to earn his, or her, daily crust. Today our nobility are not limited to safe jobs in the City but are adventurous to a degree. Jobs include pottery (Marquess of Queensberry), *restaurateur* (Viscount Newport), photographer (Earl of Lichfield), and some of them have even been known to run night clubs. But to what end?

Is it to return to the era when staff were *de rigueur*? I suspect everyone would like to have at least ten living-in staff, given that the family seat is big enough. Who would not like to rebuy the family home? Mereworth, which was built for my family and subsequently lost over the green baize in a night, is now owned by a Middle Eastern ambassador who, having no need for the money, is not likely to sell at any price. We all know where the Middle East is now (geographically speaking) but thirty years ago when style still existed, beyond the wildest dream of an ambitious débutante, hardly anyone except the Fifth Earl of Carnarvon (who sponsored the discovery of Tutan-khamun's tomb) and T. E. Lawrence knew of its exist-ence.

The Forces, or at least the Army, are considered to be very respectable employment. A commission into the right regiment (see the author's list) is an excellent way of gaining time to think before the City or factory floor. One very noble peer has been quoted as saying that the class system is perpetuated in the Army. Why not? – if it gives someone, perhaps not of noble birth, a chance to elevate himself to a dizzy height which will make him the envy of all his friends back in the mining valleys of South Wales. But there again it could cause him embarrassment when the chap is asked where his people have their country seat.

Employment is in fashion and it brings people from every stratum of society into touch with each other. That has to be more progressive than remaining INcognito and INcommunicado. Life changes, and it is rather old-fashioned to think that there are hundreds of ghastly people trying to invade a rarified community that no one really wants to admit exists. Don't they have an equal right to be there in the first place? And they probably think everyone not of their rank to be ghastly as well.

But perhaps the upper class and nobility are a separate entity. They do nothing to dispel the widespread belief that they are slightly dotty. After all, the upper classes have decided to spell their names differently and pronounce their vowels in a way that sounds as if they are attempting to speak while brushing the teeth. And if that is not confusing enough they also pronounce their names differently – e.g. Cholmondeley, Buccleuch, Beauchamp and, er, Mackwood (pronounced Mud?).

The signs are that there is going to be a huge social explosion and it is interesting to speculate what the end result will be. Could it be a closing of the ranks by the English-speaking members of Lloyd's and the syndicate at Six Mile Bottom? That would have the effect of producing an endangered species – and we all know what will happen to them, unless a John Aspinall or Sir Peter Scott gets to work. It is surely better that we all muck in together, throw away social pretentions (but hang on to our Ascot rig) and be prepared to sink a pint of mild and bitter in the pub rather than confining our imbibing to very cold dry Martinis among the élite set in Annabel's.

It all depends on what your bag is. Surely no one would turn down an invitation to Ascot (except those allergic to horses), to spend a day with a hundred of their closest friends or to mix with Royalty at a Buckingham Palace Garden Party. There are those who prefer a Cup Final, the fair ground on Epsom Heath during the Derby, or a game of darts in the local on a Saturday night.

Perhaps Mr Mackwood's book (a guide for those who want to know which are the fashionable restaurants, the IN people and the OUT, modern manners, the way to get into or keep out of gossip columns and how to social-climb) will produce a more egalitarian world. Will he go down as the greatest activist since Lenin? Give him a break, buy another copy soon, and he will be able to retire to a huge country mansion, full of staff, dogs, and gaiety. Everyone loves a millionaire ... or are they OUT?

Burghersh

Lord Burghersh

Introduction

Although I have written about the social minefield which catches out all but the deft-of-foot, I in turn realize that the publication of this book has created its own minefield. Should I go wrong, there will be the sound of an almighty explosion and I shall tumble ignominiously into a crater. I will have been found out.

The reaction to last year's *In & Out* was varied but I survived to deliberate on the tricky subject of society, and the people who form it, once again. It quite surprised me that during the year I was approached by a few people who wanted to know my reasons for dismissing their best friend/cousin/sister to the OUT column when they were such nice people; and in return thanked by some who found their names on the IN side. That answers those who doubted that this book would have any modern-day relevance – 'Who gives a damn about anything these days?' That stance is just a pretence, and you had better believe it.

In fact I was dubbed 'an incorrigible young snob' (I deny it) and yet chastised for attempting this book when my only qualification for doing so was that I worked for over four years on a national newspaper's gossip column. What better qualification, I ask myself – when the half of what was known was never written?

The same critic pointed out that I had got it all wrong by suggesting that smart people go to the *loo*. These days, it was said, really smart people trot off to the *lav*. A straw poll I conducted among my more socially aware friends came up with a group of more graphic alternatives for the lav/loo which presumably stemmed from public school and the Army. Quite a few admitted going to the loo though some proved me wrong by going to the lav – but none of them would have dared ask a friend's mother the way to the lav.

In contrast to that doubting of my knowledge on such weighty matters, others said I was eminently suited to writing on the subject – and I began thinking perhaps that was an inverted compliment.

Being something of a coward, this year I enlisted the support of a committee – although everything about committees leaves a bad taste in the mouth. The purpose of having a committee was to borrow from their knowledge rather than to form a joint opinion about which were the IN shirtmakers or ex-kings, etc. Like the author they have no wish to stick their corporate necks out (the poor fools *have*), so I have assured them complete anonymity – as the trichologist said to the patient. I must thank them for the hours they put in, although my stocks of Bollinger have never recovered. At our last meeting they insisted I write this introduction and make it clear that the following contents are my responsibility, and it is with complete honour that I accept this onerous task.

Others, too, who are less afraid to give their names, have helped in various sections. To them I extend my thanks: Lord Burghersh, Lady Elizabeth Anson, Gavin Hans-Hamilton, Laraine Ashton, Nicky Haslam, Taki, Peter Townend, Tudor Owen, Adrian Wright, Kathryn Samuel and Robert Jarman.

I can only assure the people whose names appear in this book that they should have no complaint. It is so much better to be talked about than not to be talked about – so whatever section you find yourself/your sister/cousin/best friend in, regard it as a compliment.

NEIL MACKWOOD
FULHAM, LONDON

'There are too many bourgeois colonels and budgerigars in England.'

Salvador Dali

'Whatcha, squire'

xvi

1

Snobbery

'In our own way we were both snobs, and no snob welcomes another who has risen with him.'

Sir Cecil Beaton on Evelyn Waugh

Dukes and dustmen are generally not snobs as both are devoid of social pretension. Both can dress, talk and act as they please as they are secure in their respective stations in life. True the duke, dressed in twill and tweed, might carry around a certain stateliness, but this is not to be confused with snobbery. The dustman also being without this strange affectation would never feel embarrassment if he encountered the duke on his rounds and called out to him – 'Whatcha, squire!' Most likely the duke would respond with a benign wave and a friendly smile.

Whereas the snob, who is ever-conscious of his social position and doing the right thing, would never think of addressing the duke by any other style than 'Your Grace'. Most butlers are terrible snobs and despise anyone who they believe does not match up socially with their masters. Consequently they are always trying to trip up unsuspecting guests by their overt attention. In the best houses, for instance, it is the practice for butlers to ease the dining-room chair behind one when assembling for meals. So if the form is known there should be no need to glimpse behind – but merely to detect instinctively the presence of the butler as he glides cloud-like behind you. Of course this can lead to disaster when the mischievous devil leads you to believe that he is going to perform this basic courtesy – only, you find that he doesn't, and you've sat on

1

...Only to find you've sat on thin air

thin air. The snob longs for the day when, after considerable fawning and drink-buying, he is permitted to call the
duke by his Christian name. In such cases the snob never
fails to bring into conversation the fact that 'Andrew – er,
that's Andrew Devonshire' was in sprightly form at the
club. These bores should not be tolerated and should be
discouraged by such succinct repartee as: 'That's odd,
because he told me the other day his gout was playing up.'

It is generally agreed that a snob is an unattractive
fellow and it is difficult to get anyone to actually admit
that he is a crashing snob. Most Army officers of the
cavalry and guards regiments are imbued with snobbish-
ness – indeed the Army is a snobocracy.

Those people hanging on to upper-middle or middle-
middle-class status by their fingertips also make excellent
snobs. They are not going to let go for anything and they
play life by the rules. So their god is correctness. They
never drink red wine with fish, or smoke a cigar with a
band around it, or drive a Rolls-Royce, or say 'pardon'; but
they have an impressive knowledge of *Debrett's Peerage*, go

to Ascot where they spend four days in the Brigadier Gerard Bar, and are over-lavish with their hospitality to friends who are in a position to enhance further their standing. The snob would give his right arm, and oceans of champagne, to be proposed for White's. If he has intellectual notions he will attend first nights at the opera and ballet and tell everyone that he reads Proust in French, eschews Coghill's Chaucer; his house is scattered with copies of *The Times Literary Supplement* and *Books and Bookmen*. While his manners, to people he regards as his social superiors, are impeccable to the point that they border on the nauseous, he gives himself away by being frequently rude to waiters though never to butlers. Yet everyone's idea of a snob differs and no two dictionaries seem able to agree upon a definition. *Websters* insists a snob is one who 'blatantly imitates, fawningly admires or vulgarly seeks association with those whom he regards as his superiors'. And Mr W. logically adds he is one who 'repels the advances of those whom he regards as his inferiors, one conscious of his superiority, one inclined to exclusiveness'. But here Webster goes off the rails, for surely society is an attempt at creating an exclusive atmosphere where like-minded people, pretty, rich, titled or talented, can meet and frolic in environments where the eye of the common herd is not focused in un-Christian envy.

But Webster is correct in his loathing of snobs, and concludes that they are persons 'not belonging to the upper classes – one not an aristocrat, a commoner, a plebian'. Just where this places the Earl of Lucan I am not sure. High-born, certainly; Lucky was (is?) a terrible snob whose disdain for the great unwashed is well documented and yet he selected a wife from quite a different social stratum.

Chambers partly agrees with *Websters* and opines that a snob is a person of 'ordinary or low rank; an ostentatious

3

vulgarian. One who makes himself ridiculous or odious by the value he sets on social standing or rank'. The compiler of this definition was not presumably getting in a dig at genealogists and heralds. He is probably thinking of someone like Roddy Llewellyn whose fascination for the noble backgrounds of others goes beyond the knowledge which even members of the peerage hold in their minds. The best definition of a snob comes in the admirable *Desk Standard Dictionary* of 1936 published by Messrs Funk & Wagnall of New York. They say a snob is one who 'makes birth or wealth their sole criterion of worth and is cringing to superiors and overbearing with inferiors in position, also any vulgar pretender to gentility'.

English, if not Scottish, society is less snobbish than that of our continental neighbours for the main reason that we had no real revolution to deprive the aristocracy of titles. France and Italy are riddled with bogus *comtes* and barons who really have no right to their appendages. The *Dictionnaire de la Noblesse Française*, written by Mons. de Saint Simon and E. de Sereville, concluded – after fourteen years of sorting wheat from chaff – that of the 60,000 titles used in France only some 6,700 were genuine.

For instance, one Baron Alexis de Rede, who is much revered for his party giving, art collection and Bohemian way of life, seems to have got himself a title which is not only not French but it not recorded anywhere.

The Rochanbeau family is one of the most social in France. The Marquis de Rochanbeau was one of the great American patriots along with LaFayette, but the present family, although it shares the name, is not – as far as any genealogists can define – related to the general and is therefore wittily referred to as the 'Faux Rochanbeau'.

The Italians also have a good imagination when it comes to titles. They admire ours as much as they admire our wild grouse, although genuine titles do exist. There is a well-known Italian count who married into the La

Rochefoucauld family – one of France's best. Yet there is no clue where the 'Count' found his title.

Members of French society, unlike their English counterparts, have no time for the cocktail philosophy. They share attitudes with their Belgian neighbours and circulate only among themselves – except when a great deal of money is involved. The French, like the English, married numerous millionaires in the last century but the big difference is that when a French marriage is organized, the socially inferior relations are completely ignored. Following the nuptials the poor relations are seldom (if ever) invited back to the château. There have been five marriages since the nineteenth century in the Duke de la Rochefoucauld's family, but it is reputed that most of the relations of these millionairesses have not been received after the weddings.

By many accounts some of the greatest snobs are found in that sadly deprived country Belgium. Ultra-conscious of their position, the aristocrats prefer their own company and do not entertain members of other classes. Only a small proportion of these privileged mortals retain that true arbiter of wealth – land. Most of them have sold out to industry and spend their time skiing and reminding themselves that they are of noble birth. Among the *cognoscenti* it is thought that any person with a title which does not go back before Leopold I is not a first-ranker. There is no social mobility in this land of nine million people, gassy beer, caves, EEC bureaucrats and a crumbling World Trades Fair. The old aristocracy who retain their land and style are against conspicuous consumption and leave ostentatious displays of wealth to the rich middle class. They dress discreetly which matches their social behaviour – although they lack an effective *presse jaune* to chronicle their indiscretions. Anyway, they tend to go abroad – not difficult when you live in Belgium – to have fun.

Despite the departure of the Kaiser and the formation

of a republic, Austria supports a strong upper class and nobility. Indeed, Austria is overegged with nobs – the reasons for this being twofold. With the collapse of the Empire the aristos, often penniless, scurried back to Vienna, where the more fortunate ones had land. Secondly, with every member of the family having a title there is a noticeable and automatic divide between them and the rest.

The upper middle class, as such exists in England, does not really feature in Austrian life, with the result that there is less class consciousness there. John Stonborough, a London-based journalist who has aristocratic Austrian blood coursing through his veins, attributes this to the loss of two world wars, a universally used state-school system and the enormous prosperity of the average Austrian. They are not an envious race and have a smattering of princes (Esterhazy, Schwarzenberg, Liechtenstein) and counts (Pallavicini, Traun, Harrach) to preside at their balls.

Austrians delight in shooting and especially relish invitations from British friends with grouse moors. They have a sneaking admiration for all things British and the upper crust attempt to adopt the Harris tweed, grey flannel and cravat look – which they think their counterparts are wearing here. The women tend to be of a firm disposition and plump and have a liking for Loden coats and silk scarves placed across their shoulders – sort of folksy Sloane Rangers.

Any social athlete worth his salt will be constantly dipping over to America where he may think society, class and snobbery do not exist. This is strictly not true – society of a kind can be found at such parlours as Studio 54 (now shut) and the 21 Club – which is the most fashionable restaurant in New York. Unlike England the leading and prestigious American clubs and schools are virtually unknown to the people. A large percentage of the people in this upper echelon of society need not be rich by North American standards; some will say that Paul Getty (who made his home in Surrey) was never accepted. The Rockefellers have only been accepted since the Depression and that is chiefly because of their interest in good works. The American social élite stay very much glued together, although this is changing. But it is still rare for good southern families to receive Yankees and for that matter there are very few pre-war (pre-1863) families who are received in the South. Of course there are exceptions.

The majority of names in Virginia society (yes, it does exist) are exactly the same names as found 100, 200 and 300 years ago. Look for and infiltrate the likes of: Carter, Randolph, Hill, Custiss, Washington. When President Carter's ancestry was inevitably researched there were protests from other Carters in Virginia who claimed it was impossible for the peanut farmer to be related to them since he was a baptist and came from quite another group.

A friend who recently attended a society dance in Texas found the social clock put back ten years. It was a coming-out dance and white frocks were in abundance and the term 'débutante' was used to describe the girls, who in turn talked about having 'a date' for the evening. No rogue males were allowed to upset the evening, which was taste-fully arranged. Black servants in white gloves handed around the champagne cocktails, proud moms looked on as their daughters twirled on the dance floor to the music of two swing bands. This was the quintessence of all things WASP (White Anglo-Saxon Protestant).

In Boston the names are the same as those which appear in the days of the Founding Fathers – Bradford, Winthrop, Wigglesworth, Saltenstall, Peabody, Forbes, and Amery. The Kennedy family, mistakenly regarded as America's first, are not really and truly accepted. They are Irish and memories are long among the old firm. Ambassador Kennedy bought a summer house in Cape

Cod and when his children were growing up, including the late President and the unfortunate Teddy; none of the summering children from Boston families near by were allowed by their parents to play with the Kennedy children. As one parent told the father of a friend of mine, *'Nouveau-riche*ness is not a state of mind, it's a disease which our children can catch.'

Americans from less elevated levels and with fewer pretentions are nevertheless concerned about doing the right thing, attending the right club and school – although few parents are willing to part from their young at an early age by packing them off to boarding school. But because of this state of social insecurity many Americans lives are lived in a condition of neurotic explosion (c.f. Woody Allen).

Americans must get to know not only what restaurants to frequent in order to meet the hot-shots but where to sit in them. In London it is a simple matter of sitting away from either the entrance to the street or kitchen and getting a corner seat if possible to spy on the beautiful people. But patrons of the 21 Club must know that it is important to sit on the right-hand side – to sit on the left is social death. You will be adjudged to be socially insignificant. Never take an apartment on the right-hand side of Park Avenue going uptown because the left-hand side is IN. Both are equally luxurious. Likewise, I suppose, Bayswater is perfectly comfortable but hardly chic as it is north of the park.

'So Evelyn Waugh is in his coffin – died of snobbery.'

Sir Cecil Beaton

The real French dukes

No one loves a title like the French, which is why there are so many bogus ones. Thanks to the *Dictionnaire de la Noblesse Française,* pretenders have been exposed – much to the delight of those with the real thing. Here are the top thirty-three of the *ducs*.

Uzés	Croy
Montbrazon	Poix
Luynes	Doudeauville
Brissac	Bauffremont
Rohan	Montebello
Gramont	Blacas
Mortemart	Decazes
Noailles	Albuféra
Ayen	Sabran
Harcourt	Rivoli
La Rochefoucauld/Liancourt	Magenta
Praslin	Audiffret-Pasquier
Clermont-Tonnerre	Auerstaedt
Broglie	Feltre
Lorge	Abrantès
Polignac	Otrante
Maillé	
La Force	

2

Schools – To Fag or Not to Fag?

'I don't think it did any harm. My rather meagre talent as a cook is a result of what I learnt by fagging.'

Sir John Hogg, Old Etonian Association Chairman

If there be any at all, the advantage of going to public school is that it lends the character a certain arrogance. This was a necessary quality when the youth of the nation was dispatched to govern chunks of empire in India and Africa – sometimes to have jurisdiction over an area the size of Kent. Now the atlas is no longer predominantly coloured red there are other uses for this inbuilt self-confidence which seems to fill those who attended a public school. There are scores of retired civil servants who served in the Punjab and the Congo who can tell how, single-handed, they quelled a nasty riot by simply appearing before the angry natives. These veterans will tell you that a raised hand, or in extremes a fired shot, was enough to avert violence. Such is the imperious nature acquired at public school where the boys are beaten by, and then in turn beat, other boys – given this dubious privilege by dint of being four years older.

This system, which is probably to blame for the upper classes' predilection for flagellation (remember the spanking Colonel), also encourages boys to resent their parents: 'If they loved me how could they have sent me to this place?'

Much less harmful but still character-forming is the fagging system which enables senior boys to become completely self-confident and full of hauteur by the time they

10

leave school at nineteen. This ability to feel you are superior to everybody else can be invaluable when entering certain professions (legal, commercial, politics, media), if only to intimidate the less self-confident opposition.

By attempting to keep up with the times those public schools who have abolished fagging have made a grave error and done a disservice to the pupils in their care. Servitude at a young age has many advantages – friendships between fag and fag master sometimes last a lifetime. So the finger must be pointed at Mr Michael McCrum, Eton's outgoing headmaster, who has destroyed 300 years of tradition by abolishing the system which has produced countless prime ministers, leaders and poets – although, it must be said, Percy Bysshe Shelley was never in favour of fagging.* Contrary to the wishes of some younger boys who wanted to retain the system – which in my own experience gave you access to cooking rings, endless rounds of hot buttered toast, coal fires, coffee and high-level gossip normally denied to one so junior – Mr McCrum has stopped fagging because he says he is not in favour of 'self-indulgence of this sort'. But surely one learns to command by learning to obey.

His action will deny countless Old Etonians henceforth the pleasure of recounting the tales of horror traditionally associated with public schools since the publication of *Tom Brown's Schooldays*. No more will they be able to regale wide-eyed company with stories of heating lav seats, fetching food from the tuck shop a mile away, or buying cartridges for the prefect's illicit shotgun. How sad that no

---

*For American readers. The verb to *fag* was adopted because in the mid-seventeenth century (when fagging started) it meant to toil. In America it means something completely different.

11

longer will the passages of Eton echo to the arrogant shouts of *'Boy up'* followed by the scurry of little boys competing to get to the feet of their beckoner first in order to avoid being given a task.

Girls' public schools can be just as primitive as their male counterparts and they seem to have that residual smell of polish, socks and burnt toast. Despite attempts by more ladylike members of staff to make the place look femine most girls' school defy all attempts to do this. As a result, the product of a girls' boarding school tends to be hearty and down-to-earth – which could come from sharing dormitories, and being forced to groom and wash under their ponies' tails; or from playing too robust a game of cricket or lacrosse. While the education may be of a standard superior to some boys' schools this can be conducted at the expense of femininity and Old Girls tend to greet each other with slaps to the back. Parents who have invested several thousands of pounds giving their Arabellas and Lucys a fine start in life find they have to fork out further fees to send them off to Swiss finishing schools where they will learn how to stop walking like men, how to sit elegantly and how to receive compliments from men with good grace. As far as I know there is no girls' school which supports an official fagging system but many have 'domestic science' on the curriculum – which seems to indicate that the girls are regarded as nothing much more than potential marriage fodder. ('A way to a man's heart, Desdemona, is through his stomach.')

I am in favour of service to the community, but I think the master–servant relationship is out of date and fagging survives as a relic of the past.'

Michael McCrum, Headmaster of Eton

One learns to command by learning to obey

Boys' prep schools

IN	OUT
Dragon	Temple Grove
Windlesham	Holmwood House
Stoke Brunswick	The Elms
Westminster Choir	Eagle House
Feltonfleet	St Ronan's
Mount House – Tavistock	Ashdown House
Cheam	Bilton Grange
Mowden	Hazelwood
St Aubyn's	Nevill Holt
Arnold House	Heatherdown
Sommerfields	
Ludgrove	
Eaton House	

Those which cannot be considered IN *or* OUT
Brambeltye
Colet Court
Dulwich Prep
Caldicott
Durlston Court
Haileybury Jnr

Boys' public schools

IN	OUT
Eton	St Paul's
Wellington	Stowe
Marlborough	Bryanston
Canford	Tonbridge
Malvern	Radley (over-exposed)
Sherborne	Uppingham
Felstead	Greshams
St Edward's (Oxford)	Millfield (for athletes with more brawn than brain)
Downside	
Westminster	Dulwich

14

Winchester

Stanbridge Earls (for those who failed at the above)

Milton Abbey

Ampleforth (for left-footers)

Gordonstoun

King's Canterbury

Charterhouse

Rugby

Lancing

Bradfield

Shrewsbury

The Leys

St Lawrence College

Glenalmond

Preston

St Peter's, York

Blundells

Clayesmore (despite its production of successful old boys)

Haileybury

Mill Hill

Oundle (where girls can join the CCF)

Ardingly

Brighton College

Merchant Taylors

Bedford Grammar School

Repton

Stoneyhurst College

Eastbourne

Clifton

Girls' public schools

IN	OUT
Cheltenham Ladies College	Christ's Hospital, Hertford
Wycombe Abbey	Roedean
Heathfield	Benenden
Tudor Hall	Godolphin
West Heath	Croft House
Claremont	Queen's Gate
Convent of the Holy Child, Mayfield (for left-footers)	St Mary's Ascot
	Southover
Sixth forms of all boys' public schools	Sherborne

'If you go to an English school which is run by the government, it's so bloody hot you've got to take all your clothes off, practically.'

The Duke of Norfolk

15

3

Jobs

'Generally speaking, the best people nowadays go into journalism, the second best into business, the rubbish goes into politics and the shits into law.'

Auberon Waugh

By nature young aristocrats are not the most industrious of people – in the sense that they do not enjoy the prospect of working for others. For generations people have worked for them so they feel disorientated when forced to turn up at an office every morning in order to earn a crust. The genial Earl of Longford has ascribed his nervous breakdown in the war years, when he was a second lieutenant, to the discipline he encountered when serving at that lowly rank. He says he has never liked obedience: 'Having done exactly what I wanted since I grew up I found being under orders intolerable' (quoted by Susan Barnes in *Behind the Image*).

Having to make the office at nine plays havoc with a fully lived social life, so most aristos get through that difficult period of their lives, when the inheritance has not yet come through, by getting paid for doing what is essentially their hobby. This means persuading someone to employ them to take photographs, run opera companies, to deal in fine art or wine or even greet guests at night clubs. True, some more ambitious peers are content to dabble in the City or sit behind a Sheraton desk at a merchant bank. Others who still believe firmly in the hereditary principle, and presumably in the divine right of kings, think that they have something to offer the country – so they turn to Westminster. Lord Douro, heir to the Duke of Wellington, having failed to be elected to Westminster is now a Euro MP. Others, like Lord Home of the Hirsel, have disclaimed their titles in order to enter the House of Commons; the former Prime Minister's political ambitions caused him to have three names, the Earl of Home, Sir Alec Douglas-Home, and then the final version, which is a life peerage.

Then there is the Earl of Durham, who disclaimed the title in order to further his career – only for it to falter in a recent scandal. He now calls himself Lord Lambton which, as Lady Hartwell, the wife of the proprietor of the *Daily* and *Sunday Telegraph*, pointed out, is actually incorrect.

Leaving the aspirations of peers in Parliament aside, it is a fact that the days are gone when the first son ran the estate, the second and third went into the Church or Army, and the women did nothing more than look for a husband. Nevertheless, the attitude lives on, which is why many country-bred peers envy greatly their gamekeepers who they see as having the perfect outside job.

For those of us without a Chatsworth or Blenheim to run the choice of job can be an important factor in society. It can make you interesting or it can make you appear terribly dull. It is just the chartered accountant's bad luck that he has picked a job which is best kept quiet. Remunerative it may be but it is hardly an occupation which will get them flocking around you at a party. Better to be a film producer, *restaurateur*, headhunter or something in wine, oil or fine art.

If the old taboos about working in trade have largely vanished there remains a lingering prejudice about people who open shops. But paradoxically you will find a number of children of the peerage working behind the counters of the well-known stores. Indeed, one Viscount of my acquaintance made his mark behind the counter of the wine department in Harrods – where one day he managed to knock himself out, much to the consternation of the customers. Sir James Goldsmith's son (no peer this) wished to enter the hotel trade and was last heard of in West London where he had opened a little emporium selling cigars. Such a move would have been unthinkable in any good family in pre-war days. Somerset Maugham was mortified when his wife Syrie decided to open an interior decoration shop – but then that was in the twenties and Mrs M. was the first of the society shoppies. Countless others have followed her lead without too much damage being done to their social standing. We are living in a more egalitarian age when the public are coaxed to the stately homes by lions, pop concerts and fair grounds. In the 1920s it would have been unthinkable for the remarkable Margaret, Duchess of Argyll to open up her house in Upper Grosvenor Street, Mayfair, so the public could see her bathroom, bedroom and elegant sitting room. Despite the protestations of the Grosvenor Estate who held the lease, one can only assume that all those £7.50s were needed.

'He's gone into trade, you know'

These days peers and commoners sit beside each other on boards of companies ranging from television to banking. Directorships are a convenient way of paying for trips to London and too much work is not usually necessary; while most companies will be delighted to have a title or two on their notepaper.

School-leavers should never worry about getting the right job immediately. It is a middle-class concern to agonize over one's future and it is far better to leap on a banana boat to South America than go up to the City in search of fame and success. And no school-leaver should ever take any notice of the careers advisers who are usually failed somethings-or-other – their imagination stretches only as far as the service industries. One boy at my school who had not shone academically but had scraped O-level passes in Scripture and Woodwork was seriously advised to think about a career as an undertaker. He is now something in the music world and is rather rich.

Jobs for the boys

IN	OUT
anything in wine (grower, etc.)	fashion designer
barrister	solicitor
publisher	estate agent
merchant banker	car salesman
psychiatrist	car hire
boat designer	hotelier
theatrical/literary agent	model agent
racehorse trainer	jockey (professional)
Lloyd's underwriter	property dealer
antique dealer (some)	commodity broker
film director/producer	ship broker
newscaster	stockbroker
journalist/reporter TV, radio	airline pilot
surveyor (selected firms)	doctor
sculptor/artist	graphic artist

author
squash coach
PR
interior designer
plastic surgeon
farmer (gentleman)
Church of England parson
actor
press baron
musician (classic and pop)
conductor
landscape gardener
bloodstock agent
historian
microchip technologist
biochemist
geologist
shipping line owner
glass blower
picture framer
astrologer
art investment consultant

nurse
politician
photographer (press)
tricologist
agronomist
Catholic priest
ballet dancer
conference organizer
farmer (fish)
potter
musical arranger
civil servant (except
   Foreign Office)
arms salesman
education adviser
anything in plastic
undertaker
builder
travel agent
chef (unless in France)
air steward

Jobs for the girls

IN	OUT
model	beautician
actress	secretary
charity worker	parliamentary worker
PR	*cordon bleu* cook
picture restorer	seamstress
artist/sculptor	nanny
travel writer	schoolteacher
opera singer	nurse
ballerina	club hostess
doctor	go-go dancer
art gallery work	air hostess

fashion/jewellery, etc. designer
writer
journalist
stockbroker
photographer
vet
interior designer
newscaster
diplomat
barrister
aromatherapist
fashion buyer for the better
  kind of store
don
publisher
television drama director
anything in art and antiques
choreographer
architect
antique restorer
dance arranger
bookbinder
philosopher

promotions girl (handing
  out cigarettes, etc. at
  agricultural shows)
politician
sex therapist
marriage guidance
  counsellor
dog breeder
driver
market researcher
film PA
policewoman
candlemaker
PT instructor
carpenter
cordwainer
swimming instructor
au pair
groom
barmaid
hotel worker

The Armed Forces

The Army has been dubbed the last gentleman factory, which is correct because it functions on an unquestioning hierarchical basis. Officer cadets at Sandhurst who have come from school will be bullied and cajoled by NCOs who still have to address their junior charge as 'Sir'. 'Now, then, I think you will agree that what I have seen resembles a loaded toad crossing a road – Sir!' What is it about Army men that makes them so chauvinistic when it comes to defending their regiment? Barristers do not defend their Inn of Court, public schoolboys rather apologize than stand up for their old school; but to insult a chap's regiment is to incur the wrath of a fighting man who will proceed to express himself in the way he knows best. He will trot out the numerous historic battles which his regiment won gloriously, he will point to the fact that the regiment has a member of the royal family as its colonel and that the mess-kit is the smartest worn in the Army.

In order to avoid being challenged to a duel in Hyde Park this book recognizes that there are only 'hobby' regiments and 'professional' regiments, which does not mean that one group is any less of a fighting force than the other. Many fine regiments who defend the Empire in hostile places like Belize, and no doubt cause the Russians to think twice before launching an attack on these islands, have been omitted.

For those interested in furthering a reasonable social life there are only a handful of regiments which will afford the young blood enough time to go about his nocturnal missions. To join a professional regiment will mean the likelihood of a foreign posting and less chance of raising some dust back home.

The first choice for the more dedicated socialite is the Grenadier Guards, followed by the Coldstream Guards and the Household Cavalry. The great attraction of the Grenadiers is that they are London-based and have a philosophy which allows officers to go off and pursue other interests. It is a regiment where a private income, if not essential, is encouraged because there are many expensive subscriptions to pay. No regiment appreciates mess-skinflints and failure to pay your bill can lead to terrible trouble with the colonel.

A royal equerry who was quoted by Simon Winchester in his book *Their Noble Lordships* (for legal reasons the book never came out) as saying: 'We encourage people to take their soldiering fairly lightly – we don't subscribe to the

Allows officers to go off and pursue
other interests . . .

myths of modern soldiering that you find in the recruiting
literature. It's a sort of part-time soldiering life, and that
suits a lot of people who are just biding their time until
they assume other duties later on in life. In other words,
heirs to peerages and things like that. If you haven't got
any money to speak of, then you will be perfectly welcome
to apply to become a Grenadier but you may feel a bit
bothered. If you are bothered, then we get bothered. And
then things are not too happy all round. You know what
the Grenadier Guards are like? They're rather like a nice
old London club – lots of people you know, lots of chaps
who went to your school and things. It's a most agreeable
life.'

It is a fact that the Royal Navy and the Royal Air Force
do not appeal to the modern nob or upper-class chap who
would rather join Lloyd's or a leading stockbroker where
the money is plentiful even if thrills are not. Both the

senior service and the junior have become vehicles for carrying nuclear warheads and as a result have come under the wing of the scientists and technologists. These are not suitable pastures for the frivolous but now the way is clear for the thrusting grammar schoolboy who has set his heart on flying a Jaguar rather than gaining entry to Tramp.

The RAF has changed in complexion since the days of Douglas Bader and those bewhiskered air aces. On a recent expedition to Germany I witnessed a young pilot officer and a comely WRAF officer sitting down to drinks and a meal with a group of other ranks, who felt no embarrassment or need to call the officers 'Sir'. The officers in their turn had no feelings of superiority.

Regiments

Hobby	Professional
Grenadier Guards	13th/18th Royal Hussars
Coldstream Guards	14th/20th King's Hussars
The Household Cavalry:	17th/21st Lancers
The Life Guards & The	Hon. Artillery Company
Blues and Royals	22 SAS
('Piccadilly Cowboys')	Welsh Guards
Queen's Dragoon Guards	Irish Guards
The Royal Hussars	Gurkhas
Scots Guards	The Royal Green Jackets
Kings Troop, Royal Horse	All Royal Tank Regiments
Artillery	
21 SAS (Artist's Rifles)	
Wessex Yeomanry (TA	
regiment who all seem to	
drive Range-Rovers done	
up in Army camouflage)	

The Royal Marines	The Royal Navy
The British Frontier Service	The Royal Air Force
(they look after the East–	
West German border in	
the British Area of	
Interest and number just	
sixteen	

Models

'People say that I'm offhand, tough and rude, but charming with it. I think men have been put off by the so-called glossy image I project – which mainly stems from running a model agency.'

Laraine Ashton

New York has replaced Paris and London as the fashion capital of the world, and all the top-flight model girls now come from there. English girls can still make £25,000 a year if they are in the Marie Helvin class (but there is no one else of her stature); the more average girl can earn £10,000 as a fairly ordinary clothes-horse.

It is a tough and insecure profession (trade?) and models have to be prepared to be regarded as a piece of merchandise by advertisers, art directors, photographers and agents. You are not hired for your mind, although a vivacious personality is what gets you noticed.

The days of the personality cult, when Barbara Goalen, Twiggy and Jean Shrimpton were wanted by every fashion editor and fashion designer, have gone. The work is now spread more thinly among a few dozen top names – names which mean nothing to anyone not connected with the business.

It is still a job which attracts the prettier specimens from the upper classes but if they are to last in this

25

competitive world they must have the resilience of a gossip columnist facing a libel action and have the right qualifications. Fashion writers and agents are always trying to manufacture a face of the year but predictions seldom come right. The present choice of girl has an easy personality, is curvy enough to have a cleavage, stands at least five feet nine, has matchstick legs and fits into a size ten.

Models are usually too aware of what they eat and drink and what late nights can do to the complexion to have top social value, although beauty is one of the passports to society. Very often models are not beautiful in the everyday sense but can appear so in front of a camera.

IN	OUT
Catherine Oxenberg	Clare Park
Pattie Hanson	Maudie James (failed to make the talked-about comeback)
Beverley Johnson	
Iman Hayward	
Esme Marshall	Marcie Hunt
Marie Helvin	Rachel Ward (now in films)
Jerry Hall	
Polly Eltes	Maclean twins
Cheryl Tiegs	Tessa Hewitt
Kelly Le-Brock	Simi Bedford
Janice and Debbie Dickinson	Joanne Jacobs
	Carina Fitzalan-Howard (dropped out of the game)
Michel First	
Christina and Rio Viera	
Josephine Florent	Amanda Grieve
Tara Shannon	Dathy
Margie Swearingen	Lorraine Irish
Kim Harris	Clemmy and Flora (too young to start – come back later)
Lauren Hutton (for old times' sake)	
Carol Alt	Amanda Bibby
	All male models

26

Front pages to aim for

Vogue (GB but seem to have a prejudice against home-grown girls)
Elle (France)
Harper's & Queen
Cosmopolitan
Tatler
Company

'I prefer English and Scandinavian girls to American girls. I am not mad about that fresh outdoor healthy look. I find it quite boring. I prefer a bit of mystery in my women.'

David Bailey, on his choice of models

Interior designers

IN	OUT
Nicky Haslam	Neil Zarach
Tessa Kennedy	Robin Anderson
Nina Campbell	Christopher Vane Percy
Charles Hammond	Kaffe Fassett
Colefax and Fowler	Mimmie Freyvogel of Deko 5
David Milnaric	Jean Beaudrand
Anne Peto of Images	Charlotte Clarke
Malcolm Bancroft	Albrizzi
Michael Szell	Inchbald Students
John Stefanidis	Design Decoration
David Hicks	
John Siddeley	
Mike Messinger	
Sacha de Stroumillo	

House plants are now considered to be OUT, as quite exotic foliage can be bought at Marks & Spencer and Woolworths. In their place elaborate flower arrangements or even fake blooms should be used. High-tech is not something that anyone employing any of the above should ask for. It is a dead duck mainly because people did not enjoy the sensation of sitting on tractor seats, or having their sitting rooms resemble airport waiting rooms. Comfort is IN, while fabric (hessian) on the walls is OUT OUT OUT. Striped wallpaper appears to be back IN, giving that Edwardian look. Everyone should have one intimate room, a snug, study or smoking room, painted in a seductive dark red or green. Pastels are OUT. Bathrooms should be places which lead friends to believe you spend hours in them. So they should have bookshelves, towels as decoration, sunken baths, showers, Italian or Portuguese tiles, a telephone and a couple of easy chairs. Gold taps are of little taste but a His and Hers

. . . Lead your friends to believe you spend hours
in them

basin is quite fun. There should be adequate sockets for electric razors and toothbrushes and plenty of cabinets (antique) for drugs. This is a most important room.

The sixties look should now be stripped away. This means sending all floor cushions to the jumble sale and taking the dining room table out of the kitchen and burning all macro-cookery books. The rage for opening up fireplaces goes on unabated and is to be encouraged.

Bedrooms should be warm in colour but not folksy. So all patchwork bedspreads should be ejected along with *flokati* rugs brought back from the Greek Island holiday. Thick-pile carpets in the bedroom are desirable but shag-pile numbers are overused and so OUT. Ideally men and women should not dress together as this is the time when illusions are created, so dressing rooms should be kept as such and not made into the fourth bedroom. Beds themselves should be a feature – tented ones give a mysterious Oriental flavour and are IN at the moment.

The most-erotic-bedroom prize this year goes to the former wife of a well known Middle Eastern entrepreneur. Covered in high-quality bevelled mirrors, with frescos of an ancient Greek flavour on the ceiling, it contained sockets for a home movie projector, light-dimmer switches on the bed and a panic button. One door led to the bathroom (gold taps, I am afraid), another to the main house and a third, of a more solid nature, on to the driveway. This is a little over the top and not *House and Garden* at all.

Anything made of pine (save the kitchen table) should be used to fuel that open fire as it has now outlived its fashionableness. People are turning back to the hard-woods like mahogany, and there is a revival in wooden lav seats – so much more accommodating in cold weather than icy plastic.

There is a spirit around of 'if you have it show it off'. So bring those Sheraton chairs out of the attic and put them on show and consign all Habitat stuff to the jumble sale. Paintings, while never being OUT, are now so important that rooms are being designed around them. This includes family portraits; when in the sixties and seventies it might have been embarrassing to put your past on the walls, it is now expected. Finally, it must not look as though you have paid through the nose to create the right look or visitors will detect the hand of the *nouveau* very *riche*. Everything must be done with nonchalance but it is no longer unfashionable to spend money in this way – it just must seem as though you have acted with a lack of self-consciousness.

4

The Jet Set

'The English are not egregious social climbers – they have never competed – as all they are interested in talking about is money and boffing.'

Taki Theodoracopulos

Generally speaking, the British have never competed in the 'conspicuous extravagance stakes' and are quite prepared for rich Greeks or Germans to jet around the place spreading their largess in an attempt to curry favour with people of better quality. In fact this island race (or the Anglo-Saxon element within it) tend to dismiss the jet-set mentality as being rather vulgar. One needs more money than style to entertain aboard a gin palace yacht and spend endless losing nights around a roulette wheel – and yet these two things are central to all aspiring jet-setters.

It does seem that the beleaguered British do not have much cash to throw around these days although they remain one of the most landed nations in the world. Here it has never been the thing to boast about wealth – on the contrary, one pleads poverty – which gives the rest of the world the impression that we are not good for a dime. What other nation can put up one man who owns some 300 prime acres of the capital city, as this country can? General ignorance about the rich suits the rich very well because who wants to attract the unwelcome attentions of kidnappers and the Inland Revenue whose bite can be worse than its bark?

More money than style

There have been show-offs in the past, like the magnificent Yellow Earl of Lonsdale whose fetish for his favourite colour induced him to imbibe hock at breakfast in place of tea. In living memory there have been the Dockers whose fondness for gold plate and public extravagance brought them to buy *The Shemara* – the best British motor yacht at the time. Fortunes have changed, as Lady Docker lives in social retirement in Mallorca and *The Shemara* is now in the hands of the property millionaire Harry Hyams.

It is hard to find anyone who would willingly admit being a jet-setter just as members of the lower middle class are unwilling to accept their label. Yet there is a group of people who spend more time than most of us keeping airlines solvent and who cannot claim to be full-time businessmen. They are the sybarites who often spend their lives in search of unreality among like-minded people who will not remind them that an ugly world exists outside their privileged circle. Many jet-setters need the attentions of sycophants, flunkies if you like, and in return they indulge the exorbitance of their 'guests'. The following calendar, compiled by one friend who is an international traveller and who dismisses jet-setters as being one-dimensional, is a general guide which may be followed – but the author does not recommend his readers to so do.

The jet-set year

January: Danger of all-over body tan going, so head for somewhere hot. Favourite spots Barbados, Nassau, Acapulco.

February: Time to get out of the heat and back to the snow. The glamorous bobsleigh season is under way, so back to St Moritz – a resort now full of parvenus who will be impressed with your bounteousness and the fact that you can afford to buy everyone coffee at £1 a cup.

March: The month to leave the mountains and get back to city life. Paris offers much at this time of year and Madame Regine will be waiting to relieve you of your *embarras de richesses*.

April: Time to get out of the smoke and sample Monaco where the tennis tournament is being held. It is not too late to accept Colin Tennant's invitation to spend a few days on Mustique – and you accept because Princess Margaret's house is empty and available for rent. Sunbathe on Simplicity Bay and avoid Ansecoy.

May: Once again the South of France calls. You know it is not as fashionable as it once was when Brigitte Bardot's body was a thing of wonder (not curiosity) but there is still fun to be had. Take in the Cannes Film Festival in order to complain how tacky it was. A chance to mix with the stars and entertain Peter Sellers and endless starlets aboard your Chris Craft. Monaco Grand Prix to be attended and party to be given aboard chartered yacht.

June: Back to Paris and reacquaint yourself with the door-men of Regine's, Castel's and the 78. The season is under way in London and it is a chance to don your Savile Row morning suit for the Derby and Royal Ascot ... where you pretend to know all the people in the royal carriage procession. An opportunity to give a stunning after-race party which will get widespread publicity.

July: Take in Wimbledon Final before returning to St Tropez and Monte Carlo where *le tout monde* is gathering and parading every night between six and seven at the cocktail bar in the Hôtel de Paris. A good time to show that you are a fearless gambler at the Casino and amid the *hoi polloi* in the Loews Hotel.

August: An open month which could include a trip to Hollywood to mingle with a few film stars or a tour of the Greek Islands on a yacht – which, as you know, is the only way to travel. Hope for an invitation from Stavros Niarchos to his private island off Spetsai where there is more languid game to shoot than anywhere else in the world. Cowes Regatta if you are keen to show off your new sloop.

September: A rest month for a spot of hot-air ballooning and going over the investments with the accountants. Burghley Horse Trials, Lincolnshire, for equine jet-setters.

October: New York or an away-from-it-all holiday with new lover in East Africa. Pick up new Rolls at the Motor Show at the National Exhibition Centre, Birmingham.

November: Attend Eton Wall Game to lend support to little Mustafa or Hamish. Buccleuch Hunt Ball to be attended. Top up the tan somewhere like the Seychelles or Bali and take in an opera at Sydney.

December: The month belongs to Christmas parties where none better are held – in Gstaad. Impress everyone by buying an M. Gerard bauble from the Palace Hotel where the drinks are almost as expensive. Behave badly in the

Greengo at night and ski off the hangover in the morning. Chance to entertain the Burtons with their new families and pretend not to know Gunther Sachs.

People you will meet on the way

IN	OUT
Giovanni Agnelli	Sir David Brown
Michael Pearson	Harry Theodoracopulos
Basil Goulandris	Adnan Khashoggi
The Aga Khan	M. Al Midani
Stavros Niarchos	Gunther Sachs
Martin and Nona Summers	Jean-Noel Grinda
Jackie Onassis	Christina Onassis
Robert Sangster	Harry Hyams
Ricky von Opel	Baron Steven Bentinck
Dewi Sukarno	
Baron Heinrich Thyssen	
Mick Flick	

5

The Gossip Column

'I very much regret the decline of lying. What does accuracy matter? People spend too long looking up facts.'

Amanda Grieve, model

One young peer recently admitted that he knew of Princess Margaret's friendship with Roddy Llewellyn and of the *affaire de coeur* between the then Earl of Grosvenor and Natalia Phillips well before the gossip columns got on to the trail. He added he knew more besides and expressed incredulity that so much had not been discovered by the thirsty social hounds.

On the whole the columnists – there aren't many real gossip columnists left – stick to their cast lists of publicity seekers, social extroverts, lesser members of the aristocracy, actors and others who need exposure. Rarely do the gossips delve much below the surface and almost certainly never break up a marriage – as it will have been in a shaky state by the time the hacks hear about it.

The most frequent question asked of the columnist is 'Where do you get your stories from?' It is that bogey inquiry, common to most professions, which is dreadful in its predictability. I suppose doctors are questioned about pains in the chest, commodity brokers about the price of gold, estate agents asked about the value of 'hypothetical' three-bedroom houses in Chelsea, TV producers if they know Angela Rippon, and chartered accountants ... 'Er, oh!'

The prime source of stories comes, of course, from other

journalists, a smattering of upper-class grasses who need the money, some spurned wives (remember Vivien Merchant telling the world that Lady Antonia Fraser, who had gone off with her husband Harold Pinter, had big feet?) and what the journalist euphemistically calls contacts. These are the people he spends vast amounts of his proprietors' money upon in the hope that he will glean a paragraph to take back to the office to justify a £55 lunch at the Connaught. In reality most gossip columnists operate from the office and show a distinct disinclination to go up West (End of London) to meet people. It is more fun to meet one's colleagues and bitch over a bottle at El Vino, Fleet Street's famous watering hole; a meeting which will probably be a deal more productive anyway.

To get IN

There are advantages in appearing in a gossip column – the least of which is proving to your friends that you are interesting or important enough to warrant a mention in a national newspaper column. It would be unwise to admit that you are even a little thrilled, and a definite black if you are seen in the corner newsagent attempting to buy a dozen copies of the *Daily Mail* on the day that you feature.

The person wishing to gain entry must know about the psyche of that exclusive little band of people who chronicle the peccadillos of the rich. It is hard ever to 'win' in a battle against the professional tatler because he will always have last say and endless opportunity to write about you in the most unflattering (but not libellous) manner. This will restrict you in many social situations as you will never know which is the Hickey spy or the unfaithful friend in need of £50 who will rush to the phone the moment you commit a little indiscretion. The columns have created people by constantly writing about them and giving them a public persona. This is not an enviable position in which to be – although the process of the creation may have made you the toast of London: 'He must be interesting because he's always in the papers.' Once he is gossip fodder there will be people who have never met the victim ringing up the columns when he enters a restaurant with a girl. He will never be able to misbehave in public again – and that is a considerable loss of freedom.

So learn to spot the columnist. He will almost certainly be wearing a tailored suit (if not Savile Row), Gucci shoes, a Turnbull & Asser look-alike shirt (Nigel Dempster has the real thing), and a silk tie which should match his party personality. The gossip has a terrible fear of rejection and will be flattered if you give him the time of day – especially if you possess a senior title or a particular talent. This complex that he will be shunned makes him a genial fellow with easy charm and a ready wit, the use of which he hopes will secure him a place at functions (columnists frequently attend nothing else) alongside people about whom he intends to write. His telephone manner will be plausible and it will be difficult to realize that he intends to extract a story from you while he discusses the well-being of mutual friends. He will be well informed and know more about you than you could realize because he has had access to his newspaper's cuttings library. Thus his memory is longer than yours and a three-week affair with Dai Llewellyn, which happened six years ago, will be recalled in anything that is written about you.

But you may decide a mention in one of the gossip columns will give your social life the fillip it needs. So what rules should you follow to get your name in print?

1 Be seen in the right places: Ascot, Goodwood, Berkeley Square Ball, etc.
2 Eat in fashionable restaurants (see list).
3 Patronize the fashionable clubs (see list).
4 Give an impressive party which will attract publicity.

5 Employ the right PR to publicize your party – Rogers and Cowan are the obvious choice.

6 Kiss Prince Charles at a polo match, call a press conference and explain that you are only good friends.

7 Be outrageous; throw a glass of champagne over someone famous.

8 Telephone a 'diary' and sell them some racy story about yourself. When they say Who is Minnie Smith-Whiteley? explain that she is this incredible blonde who has just hit town from LA and is a man-eater. Drop the phone, refusing to give your name but remembering to give the hacks notice of where this new find can be contacted.

9 Elope with the chauffeur.

10 Make sure you have a tag. The columnists always need a label. So be a cousin of someone with a title, an up-and-coming model/actress, a wealthy merchant banker, a movie maker, plain rich, former Davis Cup player, singer, great-grandson of an illustrious poet, be five times engaged, top amateur jockey, top choreographer, failed Tory candidate, one-time secretary to John Bentley/Sir Willian Piggott-Brown, etc., erotic artist (pornographer?), close friend of Professor Blunt/Ned Sherrin/Jeremy Norman, son or daughter of anyone famous, Old Etonian (fib about this one), miner's son, former Bunny Girl/Penthouse Pet, discharged bankrupt, fallen property dealer, ex-racing driver, stunt-man, heiress, woman executive, designer, divorcee, merry window, City whizz-kid, *restaurateur*. Anything – so long as the writer can 'identify' you.

11 Inveigle your way into the company of people who are being written about by the columnists and make a rowdy scene when a photographer is about.

To keep OUT

The majority of people in society will express public dis-approbation of gossip columns, the values they stand for, the despicable people they employ and the damage they inflict on family life. It is true gossip can harm the health – business contracts can be (and have been) lost after some unfortunate victim has appeared in the social pages swig-ging champagne with a couple of fast women for com-pany. But it is more likely to be a source of annoyance. One wealthy magnate who became a target could hardly go out on the streets of London without it being mentioned the next day. He was perhaps his own worst enemy, drawing attention to himself and occasionally getting ejected from clubs after making loud and disparaging remarks as to the class and nationality of the clients therein.

One section of society was brought up to believe that a chap did not speak to the press and it was only right to make an appearance in the public prints at birth, mar-riage and death. The gossip columnist's natural inclina-tion is to expose the kind of people who have this attitude, although he would never fill a column-inch if he was as discerning as they are. Unfortunately he must stoop to recording the foibles of lesser meat: actresses and starlets, club owners and commoners.

There is yet another group of people who protest about the 'outrageous invasion of privacy' when approached by a Paul Slickey figure and yet do not do everything to prevent their appearance in the papers. They are the 'No, sorry – no pictures' merchants who take care to present their better side to the eager lensman as they come off a plane. To be seen to be in cahoots with the gossip columnist is not what the game is about. In order to be effective the hack needs a certain distance between him and his intended victim. Some of the best gossip columnists have never conformed to the Turnbull & Asser

'No, sorry — no pictures'

shirted look described earlier, and have probably come from deprived homes in South London or Glasgow. Never having had any social standing they do not care about getting any, and, without social pretension, they only have the journalists' impetus to break the story. That type never leaves the office and his expenses reflect lengthy lunch hours around the parish of St Bride's.

The other type of columnist comes from the upper sections of the middle classes, has been to public school and drifted into gossip 'by mistake'. The life has its attractions — phenomenal champagne drinking, entrance to most clubs, parties, and trips to Monaco, Barbados, Gstaad and New York. Any ordinary person would have to be on £30,000 to sustain such a lifestyle.

However, there is a price to pay for all this extravagance. The eating out makes you fat, while the rich food reacts with the chemicals produced from worrying about filling the empty space five days a week. The constant

41

imbibing of decent bottles of champagne blurs values, and the gossip columnist will expect the best of everything in private and public life. This causes a state of bankruptcy although do live the life of Adnan. Home life will not flourish but cynicism will, which covers up what Richard Compton Miller of the *Evening News* has called 'a brittle job satisfaction'. Such is the nature of the men who plague the rich and the powerful, the stupid and the beautiful who make up the motley social scene. How do you keep out of their sights?

1 Avoid all fashionable restaurants but stick to more sober places like the Mirabelle, the Connaught, La Gavroche. Most hacks' expense accounts will not stretch that far.

2 Do not go to night clubs where *papparazzi* (street photographers) hang about. Annabel's is safe but Tramp probably is not.

3 Have loyal friends and never tell acquaintances too much.

4 Appear boring, at least to the columnists. Put it around that you don't bet, don't smoke and only drink in moderation. Example: the Duke of Westminster, who is a pillar of respectability.

5 Don't turn up to the first day of Ascot with a flashy girl on your arm.

6 Refuse invitations to club openings/first nights where photographers and writers will be *en force*.

7 Become very dear and personal friends with proprietors of the world.

8 Hire a PR and refer all press calls to him.

9 Train servants to say nothing to the press.

10 When caught by the hack on the telephone, affect a

butler-like voice and say: 'Sorry, sir, his Lordship/Grace is not at home.' Or, like one well-known duchess, simply say could they hold on for a minute, go off and prune some roses, return in twenty minutes and express surprise that they are still holding on. Repeat the process.

11 Point out that the story is untrue and say you employ top counsel so they had better get it right. Gossip columnists are not that frightened by writs, so don't threaten them too much.

12 Keep your nose clean.

The cast

IN

Daily Mail diary: ex-incumbent Nigel Dempster stepped down because he was no longer ejected from parties from the fifth floor. He could be back.

Daily Express: William Hickey – former spear-carrier Peter Tory hides behind the pseudonym.

London *Evening News*: Richard Compton Miller, son of a judge.

London *Evening Standard*: diary run by thrusting team headed by charming art-deco collector.

Sunday Express: Town Talk, run by *Private Eye*'s fragrant hackette Lady Olga Maitland – daughter of the Earl of Lauderdale.

OUT

Sunday Telegraph: Albany – safe establishment stuff. Mandrake, where-else-can-we-put-it slot.

Sunday People: cuttings job.

London *Evening Standard*: Emma Soames' column. Not really a gossip column, more of a diary which plays safe.

Daily Telegraph: Peterborough – the column with the funniest tailpiece but not in the gossip column stakes.

The Times and *Guardian* diaries: both erratic and low on gossip.

Harper's & Queen: Jennifer – would be the first to admit she is not a gossip

News of the World: Whitefriar's Diary. Downmarket stuff, this, run by a former William Hickey with a fondness for caviar.

Sunday Times: Atticus, by Stephen Pile. Lacks style since departure of Prince Charles's biographer Anthony Holden.

Ritz: Alice French, new to the game but shows promise and cheek by taking along own camera to private parties.

columnist, more of a Boswell to the people who she (Betty Kenward) thinks are important.

'It works. Once your name has appeared in a gossip column you will automatically be invited to future embassy and house parties.'

Rozanne Weissman of Washington, who for £6 gives classes in the art of social climbing

'. . . good conversation is brewed in relaxation among friends, laced with booze and mischievousness. It is compounded of scurrility, and gossip, and silliness, and slander . . . and it's not designed for mass consumption.'

Alan Coren, editor of Punch, *on chat shows*

'They fulfil an essential function – one which would be dangerous to suppress. It wouldn't destroy the appetite for gossip if you did.'

Auberon Waugh on gossip columns

6

People

'People only send me invitations now because they want
to say they've met the notorious Lady Lucan.'

The Countess of Lucan

Society is about socially motivated groups of people who,
because they have something in common, like to gather
together to amuse and entertain each other. The society of
the twenties and thirties was much better defined than it is
these days as open displays of wealth and breeding were
not frowned upon as they are inclined to be today. The
war was a great leveller and threw together people of all
classes, doing much to break down the secret wall which
surrounded the overprivileged. But perhaps the wall has
not been entirely demolished and even in the 'enlightened
eighties' the senior ranks remain unbroken and those of
lower birth and ability have still not been admitted.

There are various levels of society – the people who
regularly entertain in their houses and surround themselves with what could be termed an establishment crowd.
This means cultivating people from the worlds of the
senior civil service, politics, the arts and the diplomatic
service.

That crowd are hardly likely to mix with the group of
people who patronize Tramp – although a fusion of both
might be found at Annabel's where roués and rulers like to
go to feel exclusive and safe from the swivelling eyes of
gossip columnists who, in theory, are banned from the
'exclusive' Berkeley Square basement.

The younger set who use London as their capital and

enjoy going out and being seen are a blend of 'common and class' – wherein the hairdresser (actually, last year's flavour), the PR, the publisher, the rock musician and the peer mix more or less happily together.

In the first edition of this book I wrote that people collect people along with antiques and pictures. They do. The successful hostess is one who can open her address (contacts) book and draw upon a selection of the most fascinating people in London. You should be able to call upon Norman St John Stevas and invite him to dinner alongside Jarvis Astaire or Edna O'Brien and the Countess of Harewood.

Contrary to belief, people from different backgrounds enjoy meeting one another, and careful matching is not as important as it once was. Nevertheless, it would be dangerous to throw one group together with its opposite, because both sets would feel threatened by each other's values.

Dukes

IN
Westminster (plain nice)
Sutherland
St Albans (fun)
Rutland (unwitting coal magnate?)
Roxburghe (grand)
Devonshire (grander)
Buccleuch (grandest)
Argyll
Beaufort (stately)
Norfolk (Tory rebel?)

Marquesses

IN
Bath (despite going into trade)
Bristol
Bute

46

Cholmondeley
Dufferin and Ava
Hertford
Londonderry
Milford Haven (see Debs' delights)
Northampton
Queensberry
Salisbury
Blandford
Hartington
Granby

Earls

IN	OUT
Alexander of Tunis	Lucan (missing,
Bathhurst	presumed
Cadogan	living)
Cawdor	
Denbigh	
Derby	
Harewood	
Howe	
Lichfield	
Lonsdale	
Mansfield	
Normanton	
Pembroke	
Selborne	
Shaftesbury	
Snowdon	
Spencer	
Westmorland	
Rocksavage	
Jermyn	

Viscounts, barons and bearers of courtesy titles

Astor
Bridport
Cobham
Cowdray
De L'Isle
Hereford
Leverhulme
Long
Monckton
Norwich
Portman
Rothermere
Petersham
Weymouth
Vestey
Brabourne
Camoys
Carrington
Harlech
Henley
Hesketh
Howard de Walden
Mancroft
Melchett
Montagu of Beaulieu
Mowbray, Segrave and Stourton
Parmoor
Reay
Rendlesham
Rothschild
Strathcarron
Tollemache
Tryon
Windlesham
Seymour

Greenock
Burghersh
Cranbourne

Hostesses

'I like society hostesses. They make things happen – well, the good ones do. They spend all their lives arranging parties, deciding you should meet interesting people.'

Andy Warhol

IN	OUT
Princess Michael of Kent	Viscountess Rothermere
Countess of Dufferin and Ava	Fleur Cowles
Mrs Serena Balfour	Mrs Ruth Fitzgibbon
Linda Heathcote-Amery	Countess of Dudley
Tessa Kennedy	
Mrs Robin Hambro	
Lady (Sonia) Melchett	
Melissa Wyndham	
Sybil, Marchioness of Cholmondeley	
Marquerite Littman	
Baroness (Gaby) Bentinck	

Bachelor and gentleman hosts

IN	OUT
Andrew Ward-Jackson	John Stephanides
Nicky Haslam	David Frost (who
Simon Sainsbury	entertains mainly
John Bowes-Lyon	for business reasons)
(New York and London)	Lord Weidenfeld
Christopher Gibbs in the	Lord Goodman
country	Ted Heath
Michael White (when in town)	Rocco Forte
The Philippines Ambassador	

Mark Birley (mainly in his
   clubs)
Lord Parmoor
Charles Harding
Guy Neville
Norman St John Stevas
   (admire his papal regalia)
Gavin Henderson
John Aspinall
Sir Hardy Amies
Walter Lees
Aziz Radwan

Girls unlikely to be queen
Lady Jane Wellesley
Davina Sheffield
Lady Camilla Fane
Sabrina Guinness
Catherine Oxenberg
Lady Rose Neville
Any American
Lady Sarah Spencer (on
   account of her recent
   marriage to Neil
   McCorquodale)
Mrs Jane Ward (or any
   other divorcee)

Girls still in the running
Amanda Knatchbull
Edwina Hicks
Princess Nora of
   Liechtenstein
Princess Marie Astrid
   (despite Buck H's
   denials)

Ex-kings

A delightful group to which to belong, although the
following would not probably agree.

IN
Constantine of Greece
   (based in Hampstead)
Sultan of Zanzibar (the

OUT
Bokassa (the deposed
   despot in the white
   Guccis)

admirable Seyyid Jamshid bin Abdullah is reputed to keep a little court in Portsmouth)

Umberto of Italy (Portugal-based)

Leka of Albania (expelled from Spain for having his own arsenal of guns – now in Zimbabwe)

Michael of Romania (represents American and British firms)

Prajadhipok of Siam (looks nothing like Yul Bryner)

Otto von Hapsburg, formerly of the Austro-Hungarian empire (now a Euro MP for West Germany and has no pretentions)

Rechad of Tunisia

Simeon of Bulgaria

Prince Alexander Karageorgevich, pretender to the Yugoslav throne (a Chicago accountant who says if called upon will gladly step into the shoes of President Tito)

OUT

Bokassa (the deposed despot in the white Guccis)

former Shah of Iran

Comte de Paris (de Gaulle used to tease him by calling Henri d'Orléans 'Your Royal Highness')

Grand Duke Vladimir (claimant of all the Russias)

Prince Tomislav of Bulgaria

Idris of Libya (Cairo-based)

'If there could be a second Jesus Christ in the world – he would be the second one.'

*Princess Ashraf Pahlavi, the twin sister of
the deposed Shah of Iran, on her brother*

Millionaires

IN	OUT
Ravi Tikoo	Kerry Packer
Algy Cluff	Christina Onassis
Daniel K. Ludwig	Bunker Hunt and *frère*
Stavros Niarchos	*Mahdi al Tajir*
Duke of Westminster	*Lord Kagan*
Sir Arnold Weinstock	*M. al Midani*
Sir Charles Forte	*Adnan Khashoggi*
Peter Cadbury	*Harry Hyams*
Lord Rothschild	*Sir David Brown*
Lord Vestey	*Paul Mellon*
Giovanni Agnelli	*Gunther Sachs*
Sir James Hanson	*King Khalid*
Baron Heinrich Thyssen	*The Aga Khan*
Nigel Broackes	*Hugh Heffner*
Lord Romsey	

Gucci socialists

By definition a Gucci socialist need not wear the distinctive Italian footwear so beloved by those who seek the symbols of success. But *he* will probably have a wardrobe full of tailored pinstripe suits and *she* will be careful not to patronize the more obvious *haute couture* houses but will dress in style. They are capitalists in socialists' clothing, and although he might have been sent to public school, and would like to give his children a good start in life by sending them there as well, he is unable to do so because it would not be consistent with his public image of a man with the common touch. No élitist he – but he is not beyond moving into an area where there is a good comprehensive school like Holland Park.

He can put his convictions behind him to suit his will (such as twice a year when the share dividends come in) and sees no great wrong in collecting rent from any property he may have – which, after all, is his inheritance.

The Gucci socialist is an appreciator of the good life and he is able to justify a standard of living although this is quite out of the reach of the people about whom he professes to show concern.

He need not be a member of the Labour Party but at some stage he probably was. Militant unions are something of an embarrassment to him, although he can blame their actions on a intransigent Tory Government. Often the Gucci socialist will have joined the Labour movement because it is thought progress to the top is swifter there than in the Conservative camp. Anyway, his or her public school background would not have been so noticeable there – and you need to get noticed in politics.

Gucci socialists are careful to take up residence in seemingly unfashionable areas like Battersea and the East End of London. This is so they can boast that they live South of the River and in the East End – the fact that they have 'Prince of Wales Drive' and 'Georgian Limehouse' as addresses, with views over the park and the River Thames, makes no difference.

Gucci socialists?

Lord Longford
Lord Weidenfeld
Shirley Williams
Lord Gifford (pronounced Jifford)
Dolly Burns
Lord Kagan
Peter Jay
Brian Walden
David Owen
Tony Benn
Lord Lever
Baroness Falkender
Robert Robinson
Lord George-Brown

Roy Jenkins
Woodrow Wyatt

Businessmen who made it – according to The Times
Tiny Rowlands (IN)
Nigel Broackes (IN)
Sir James Hanson (INish)
Lew Cartier (ex-butcher's boy who amassed a £10 million
    fortune) (OUT)
Phil Harris (carpets – OUT)
Ernie Harrison ('the decade's most successful
    industrialist') (IN)
Cyril Spencer (OUT)
Sir Alex Jarratt (IN)
James Gulliver (OUT)
Gerald Ronson (OUTish)
Maurice and Charles Saatchi (IN and IN)

Photographers

IN	OUT
Helmut Newton	David Hamilton
Alice Springs	Tom Hustler
David Bailey (fashion)	Brian Duffy
Barry Latagan	Terry O'Neill
Lord Snowdon	Erica Creer
Lord (Patrick) Lichfield	Pat Booth
Desmond O'Neill (society)	Viscount (Derry) Moore
Barry Swaebe (society)	Tim Page
Bill Bates (society)	Ron Gallela (and all
John Bishop	*papparazzi*)
Steffano Massimo (fashion)	Brian Duffy
Lorenz Zatecky	Gina Lollabrigida
Tony McGhee	Charlotte Rampling
Richard Young	
(not as a writer)	
Don McCullin	

Norman Parkinson
Alex Chatelain
Neil Kirk
John St Clair
    (alternative society)
Sir Geoffrey Shakerley

Film directors

IN	OUT
Malle	Cimino
Ford	Edwards
Coppola	Lean
Roeg	Preminger
Losey (*père et fils*)	Nichols
Donner	Winner
Schlesinger	Bertolucci
Scorsese	Anderson
Allen	Forbes
Loach	Jones of *Python*
Jarman	Nelson
Fassbinder	Siegel
Ray	Peckinpah
Scott	Eastwood, Clint
Parker	Stallone, Sylvester
Bogdanovich	Roddam
Yates	
Ross	
Fellini	
Donan	
Forman	
Jewison	
Kubrick	
Polanski	

Mummers

IN	OUT
John Wood	Patrick Mower

Helen Mirren

Tom Conti

John Hurt

Paul Scofield

Timothy West

Dudley Moore

Hywel Bennett

Nastassia Kinski

Derek Jacobi

Hugh Burden

Robert Hardy

Maria Aitken

Leonard Rossiter

Michael Jayston

Sir Alec Guinness

Glenda Jackson

Patrick Magee

Prunella Scales

Annabel Leventon

Yul Brynner

Carmen Du Sautoy

Zoe Wanamaker

Jane Asher

Tom Courtenay

Jill Bennett

Paula Wilcox

Ian Ogilvy

Lorraine Chase

John Standing

Ian McShane

Sian Phillips

Diana Quick

Maureen Lipman

Donald Pleasence

Beryl Reid

Pat Phoenix

Benny Hill

Eric Sykes

Lalla Ward

Ron Moody

Richard Johnson

William Franklyn

Keith Michell

John Le Mesurier

Richard Briers

Paul Eddington

Peter O'Toole

Fiona Richmond

Reg Varney

Simon Williams

Hugh Paddick

Joan Collins

John Cleese

Michael Caine

Gerald Harper

Prunella Gee

Susan George

Anthony Andrews

Alex. ndra Bastedo

Diana Dors

Robert Powell

Olivier Tobias

Thora Hird

Linda Lou Allen

Sheila Hancock

Ringo Starr

Bianca Jagger

Edward Fox

Artists

IN	OUT
Wyeth	Warhol
Heron	Bacon
Organ	Lowry
Hockney	Armitage
B. Bogdanovich	B. Cooke
D. Ker	E. Halliwell
N. Waymouth	Topolski
Procktor	
Freud	
J. Arp	
Hepworth	
Moore	
Keating	
Fink	
Turnbull	
Paolozzi	
Coldstream	
Uglow	
Bratby	
Buhler	

'Life is happier if it is full of pretty people.'

Jilly Cooper

The team

IN	OUT
Mark Shand	Victor Lownes
Lord Burghersh	Dai Llewellyn
John Bowes-Lyon	Michael Dupree
Nicholas Soames	Jeremy Browne
Lady (Bindy) Lambton,	John Paul
daughters and son Ned	Steven Bentinck (absent)
Benjy Fraser (absent)	Marilyn Cole

Marquess of Blandford
Lady Teresa Manners
(her ball at Belvoir
was one to get to)
Jonathan Hope
Hugo Guinness
Ned Ryan
Esmond Cooper-Key
Davina Phillips
Richard Northcott
Davina Sheffield
Miranda Guinness
Colin Tennant
John Bentley
Jose Olivestone
Valentine Lindsay
Simon Ackroyd
Lyndall Hobbs
Clio and Dido Goldsmith
Gerald Harford
Branco Bokun
Peter 'Petty' Coates
Christopher Balfour
Mark Birley
Michael Pearson
Rupert Deen
Emma Soames
Laraine Ashton
Lady Caroline
Cholmondeley
Rebecca Fraser
Tara Tooth
Tracy Chamoun
Lord Neidpath
Flora Fraser
Eric Wachmeister

Jane Stonehouse
Charles Riachi
George Moreton
Aldine Honey
Viviane Ventura
Cyril Stein
Tommy Sopwith
Sabrina Guinness
Mynah Bird
John Reid
Bianca Jagger
Prince Ali Mushidabad
Paloma Picasso
Andrew Logan
Angie Bowie
Dana Gillespie
Nicholas Monson
Prince Stash Stanislaus
Roberto Shorto
Giancarla Forte
Arianna Stassinopoulos
Venetia Spicer
Kit Hunter-Gordon
Tessa Dahl
Hylan Booker
Jonathan Bulmer
Ben Coleman
Christopher Cole
Kim Smith-Bingham
Mark Thatcher
Mark Swire
Melody Wilson-
Macdonald
Martin Amis
Peter Langan
Mark Agar

Cosima Vane-
  Tempest-Stewart
Anita Guinness
Lady Edith Foxwell
Billy Keating
Vanessa Hedley
Cosmo Fry
M.&N. Summers
Mark Boxer
Amanda Dallas
Marie-Louise Lascelles
Lady Carina Fitzalan-
  Howard
Charles Palmer-
  Tomkinson
Clare Hambro
Johnny Ramsay
Phillipe Niarchos
Andrew Parker-Bowles
David Somerset
Christopher Sykes
Chessie Thyssen
Lady Jane Wellesley
Lord Alexander Rufus
  Isaacs
Prince/ess George Galitzine
Homayoun Mazandi
Lady Silvy Thynne
Pandora Stevens
Sarah Gordon Lennox
Sophie Hicks
Henrietta Calder-Smith
Louise Huntington Whiteley
Charles Delevigne
Lucy Fox
Benjy Clutterbuck

Nathan Gelber
Roddy Llewellyn
Michael Fish
Chantal d'Orthez
Jonathan Aitken
Natalie Hocq
Lord Anthony Rufus
  Isaacs
Marella Oppenheim
Robin Courage
Charles Mackenzie Hill
Peter Hoos
Tom Gilbey
Michael Doxford
Andy Warhol
Halston
Diana Vreeland
Grace Coddington
Dee Wells
Baron Arnaud de Rosnay
Sir William Piggott-Brown
Daniel Topolski
Vidal Sassoon
Janet Street Porter
Michael and Tina Chow
James Baring
Roman Polanski
Prince Ernst of Hanover
Harold Fielding
Françoise Pascal
Ron Kass
Imogen Hassall
Dee Harrington
Duffo
Michael Roberts
Britt Ekland

Lady Charlotte Curzon
Lord Hesketh and brothers
Amanda Aspinall
Alain Chevasseur
Lord (Charles) Greenock
Caroline Blackwood
Lady Elizabeth (Liza)
    Campbell
Charlotte Gordon-
    Cumming
Brian Alexander
Colin Tennant and Lady Anne
Nicholas and Victoria von Preussen
Lady Royston (absent)
Lady Francis Russell
Sandy Harper
Andrea von Strumm
Marie-Noelle Dreesmann
Prince Kiko Hohenlohe
Joanna Naylor-Leyland
Fiona Heathcote
Consuelo Fraser
Rupert Everette
Lady Mary Gaye Anstruther-Gough-Calthorpe
Steve Strange
Amanda Grieve
Lady Hartwell
Anthony Mackay
Princess Joan Aly Khan
James Hunt

David Shilling
Nat Cohen
Larry Adler

7

What's in a Name?

Names should be different or plain appealing but never hackneyed or too self-conscious (Torquil, Jasmin, Jason). Pop-stars like their children to have names with an ono-matopoeic appeal (Zak, Zowie, Jade) while the lower classes have a tendency to shorten names to make them sound less formal (Bill, Fred, Dave, Pete, Dick) but this is not confined to their class. The upper classes sometimes go over the top in an attempt to be original in their choice of names (Peregrine, Flora, India, China), but they tend to find names which, being of one syllable (Neil, John, Mark, Roy, James, Jane), cannot be abbreviated. The choice of names is arbitrary and connotation has much to do with selection – my kind, gentle Melanie is your snake-haired Medusa. Since we have lost respect for our public leaders and are no longer in awe of celluloid figures it has gone out of fashion to name one's children after these people – so there will be no mass registration of Meryls and Maggies or Jimmys and Dustins. The main criterion in choosing a name for children is to be kind; imagine being stuck with one of those names which when en-countered always brings on a snigger. Going to the bother of changing names by deed poll is a little shaming.

	Boys
IN	OUT
Robert	Kenneth
Ned	Arnold
Alexander	Norman
Roy	Geoffrey
Charles	Luke

Matthew	John
Mark	Melvyn
Harry or Harold	Julian
Patrick	Algernon
Hugh	Jason
Karl	Desmond
Ian/Iain	Sebastian
Neil	Gervaise
Jeremy	Eric
Peter	Bill
Tatton	Victor
Guy	Roland
Alastair	Joseph, Joe
Cecil	Lew
Michael	Tarquin
Christopher	Pearson
Tom	Warren
Richard	Nigel
Douglas	Robin
Frederick, not Fred	Clive
Rupert	Lee
Ralph	Sidney
Edward	Egon
Andrew	Leroy
Philip	Jade
Jonathan	Harvey
Adam	Herbert
George	Bert
William, Willie	Ludwig
Hamish	Daniel
Toby	Marmaduke
Sam	
Oliver	

Girls

IN	OUT
Natassia	Sonia
Claudia	Melita
Camilla	Hilary
Davina	Bianca
Melanie	Blanche
Catherine	Pamela
Elizabeth	Anne
Jilly	Mynah
Anna	Kim
Marie-Louise	Flo
Alexandra	Marcia
Eleanor	Janet
Joan	Hilary
Charlotte	Maureen
Susanna	Gaia
Sophia	Tara
Louisa	Selina
Sara, Sarah	Margaret
Amanda	Nona
Joscie	Josephine
Flora	Beatrice, Beatrix
Antonia	Marguerite
Nicola	Polly
Emma	Marie
Felicity	Jerry
Carolyn	Valentina
Christina	Lillie
Rachel	Erica
Frances	Kate
Tessa	Harriet
Serena	Arabella
Victoria	Drusilla
Hannah	Susan
Jessica	Sheila

Ingrid

Chloe

Lucy

Pippa

Gayle

Clare

Beryl

Brigid

Martine

Nicknames to drop

(If you know their identity count yourself IN.)

'It annoys me enormously. "Bubbles" to me is someone who is a very frothy character; basically I'm a very serious person.'

Lady Rothermere, on her nickname

Bunter

Brookie

Boofy

Bubbles (there's more than one)

Bobo

Brian

Binky

Bear

Beasty

Bunny

Bengy

Chalky

The Bishop

Demi-Monde

Fish & Chips

Goldilocks

Jaws

Piranah Teeth

Pongo

Piggy

Puffin

Pope

Seducer of the Valleys
Sharon
Sir Reginald Bullying-Manner
Rollo
Thoroughly Unscrupulous
Porchey

'It hurts me when I am labelled The Seducer of the
Valleys – Dai Lock-up-your-daughters.'

Dai Llewellyn

Ambitious mothers and their apathetic daughters

8

Débutantes – Do They Exist?

'I don't know how to describe them . . . a lot of City gents,
but young, and a lot of soldiers.'

'Deb of 79' – Henrietta Calder-Smith, on deb's delights

It was left to a night club to put on a competition to select
the 1979 Deb of the Year in place of the more traditional
testing ground that was the Season. The self-appointed
Master of Ceremonies was that ex-deb's delight Dai
Llewellyn, who thought up the wheeze to lend some
publicity to the night spot where he 'works' (*sic*). The
debs, none of whom knew anything of the formal white
ball gowns once worn by their predecessors, unless perhaps they had stolen a glance at their mother's photo-
graph album, were examined on eating caviar and pop-
ping champagne corks – something which any deb know-
ing her place would leave for the butler to do. All this was
carried out in front of a panel of personalities like Reginald
Bosanquet ('I've been accused of making the news as well
as reading it').

The tacky contest is a long way from the original ritual
which debs went through in the days when it really meant
something, i.e. being presented at court. Since that once-
invaluable piece of snobbism has been stopped the whole
deb scene is an empty charade acted out by ambitious
mothers and their apathetic daughters.

These days the season limps on, beginning in April with
the Berkeley Dress Show and a lively cocktail party given

by the 'Deb Man' Peter Townend. Not to get on Mr Townend's list means to be excluded from the events of the season; and failure to be invited to model at the Berkeley Dress Show is to be relegated to the second division. Although there is a paucity of good London events there has been something of a revival of more lavish country entertaining. But there is no reason to believe the whole deb caboodle is, once again, about to take off.

Whereas there is no shortage of mothers wishing to thrust their daughters into/onto society the old proving grounds for debs have vanished. The Queen Charlotte Ball, where eager young men so gleefully emptied their pockets of white mice upon the dance floor, has folded, as has the Pied Piper Ball. Apart from a few shared cocktail parties and half a dozen unexciting tea parties, when the debs reputedly scour the room for an eligible suitor, the veils have been drawn over the London season.

Even Betty Kenward, who as Jennifer in *Harper's & Queen* magazine plays a Boswell-like role by chronicling every society event, no longer publishes a list of deb dos. Indeed, she says the scene is not what it used to be, although she makes *en passant* references to various girls 'coming out'. Alas, in a much more cynical age the phrase has been taken away from the debs and put to use by quite another group of people. The days when debs feared for their honour and wondered if their escorts were NSIT (not safe in taxis) has passed by with the mass manufacture of the pill and the cultural revolution (sexual?) which came in the sixties. It is now a case of NSIBMW – more of a reference to the young man's driving than to his libido. Let Henrietta Calder-Smith's mother have the last word:

'In my day the Season was really for the aristocrats. Now, of course, the aristocrats have no money. So the Season's got terribly commercial. It's a way for families who don't know anyone to introduce their daughters to people. The aristocrats know everyone anyway. If money's no object you can have a wonderful time.'

'Henrietta is a very pretty and lively girl. I'd say that she was my favourite deb, although one shouldn't really have favourites.'

Peter Townend, social editor of Tatler, and chief deb master, on 1979 'Deb of the Year' Henrietta Calder-Smith

Debs	*Delights*
Vanessa Percy	Marquess of Milford Haven
Fiona Golfar	Lord Howland
Edwina Tatham	Julian Metcalfe
Serena Franklin	Mark Cecil
Lady Marcia Leveson-Gower	
Edwina Hicks	

9

Language

'Any belted earl under fifty will talk quite naturally about being *skint* when he is short of lolly, of having a *kip* and being *conned*.'

Dicky Buckle

While it really does not matter if you don't speak quite like the Queen does, there is no doubt that language and diction remain class and social indicators. Language like society is in a continuous state of change and to be hip (OUT) one must keep in touch with the latest expressions and reject those which were yesterday-speak.

Somebody called Lord Kings Norton recently opened a debate in the House of Lords about the deterioration of the English language. He complained, rightly, you may agree if you are a stickler for such things, that too many people now use *commence* when they mean start and *donate* when they mean give. And that the influence of language from America is leading us to use longer words where shorter ones would do; *apartment* for flat, *assignment* for job and *location* for place. The well-intentioned Lord K.N. presumably was not aware of the essential need for change and movement or of the desire to create identity through the use of language.

It might have been hip to say you were searching for an apartment in the early sixties but certainly the word has now outlived its usefulness. One now lives in a duplex. In the same way no one goes on vacation – although they used to. More acceptable people now go on leave or take a short break or tour and they probably pop down to Monaco, which sounds much more casual.

Following publicity in *Private Eye* no one complains that they are in 'an ongoing no-job situation' – unless they are having a spot of linguistic fun.

After the war it was fashionable for the upper crust to emulate the cockney slang of their employees: 'I must get me 'orse saddled, crikey, oh Gawd, drop dead, etc.' The aping of cockney seems to be dropping away – probably because we now have the 'real McCoy' in society. Instead there is a tendency to talk Northern – the Parkinson-Hartyese of Lancashire and Yorkshire.

In more fertile times when gels had it all their own way society almost invented a language of its own. It was the language of the bright young things documented by that not-quite-a-gentleman Evelyn Waugh. Its purpose was to create a special élite who were privy to its meaning to the exclusion of those who did not belong. Secret languages are nothing new and in history their purposes have always been exactly the same. The type of speech uttered by P. G. Wodehouse's amiable buffoon Bertie Wooster ('Absolute rot, what, by Jove!, got a pippin' idea, old bean, topping, a deuced brainy sort of fellow, be a sportsman, rather, old top') is all discovered now and *démodé*.

It has been replaced by the less romantic and narcissistic vernacular called psycobabble, which is intended to convey the feeling that we all have terrible problems coping with life – rather than the more attractive stance which Bertie Wooster took (although he *was* always getting into a terrible mess). His Jeeves, who inevitably came to the rescue, has been replaced by a language which cannot be pinned too closely to real meaning. Reay Tannahill has dubbed this new lingo 'gobbledegook and gobble-de-guru' in her book *Sex in History*. She reckons it has been the salvation of twentieth-century man, and it is the Americans (whose invasion of our culture is whole-sale) who have brought it to public notice; or more specifi-cally the Californian Americans who are not unnaturally covered in guilt – surrounded as they are by blue skies, rampant consumerism, beautiful bodies and the worship of success. In other words the good life has got to them – and the only direction is a retreat either on to the psy-chiatrist's couch or into a language which indicates that 'here I am, an individual attempting to answer the ques-tions, where did I come from, why am I here, what am I going to?' Hollywood is not called Tinsel Town for noth-ing, although it is part of the horrendous urban sprawl of Los Angeles with its laid-back inhabitants, predatory females, fat cats, status symbols and smog. It is a land where the hang-up is as common as the hangover, which explains why a centrefold girl in a recent issue of *Playboy* magazine was reputed to have said: 'Believe it or not, I have no sexual hang-ups whatsoever. Sexual hang-ups are for the birds.' Golly! The poor girl must have had a happy childhood in an unbroken family – and that could be a disadvantage down California way.

Surely there is no other land where the deeply confused can purchase a book by one Everett L. Shostrom entitled *Becoming a Self-Actualized Person* or even Hayden Curry's *Improving Your Skiing*, which unfolds the secrets of mental exercises designed to relax skiers and maintain self-confidence on difficult slopes. Of course society is a diffi-cult slope and the need to maintain one's self-confidence is indeed important, but recourse to a guide is not really the way ahead. But I digress.

Language is an instinctive thing and one should be at ease with it. It is silly to try to be what you are not, because sooner or later the unconcealed traps which are inadvert-ently placed in the way of the climber will find out and ensnare the impostor.

Whereas in the past every actor went through the

72

gentrification process that was RADA (as a result their working-class accents were painful to behold), entrants to the Thespian art now come from every station in life. Although the BBC allows its broadcasters on the air with understandable regional accents (the Gorbals and the Isle of Dogs are yet to be represented) it still must be said that it is no disadvantage to speak in a way which distinguishes you as a public school man (woman) as distinct from a direct grant person. The overblown voice, the product of one too many elocution lessons, is not to be encouraged as it tends to sound phoney. It is impossible to say whether Mrs Thatcher or Ted Heath have spent many agonized hours trying not to snuff out a candle as they annunciated the names of those three gorgeous counties Hampshire, Hertfordshire and Herefordshire, but it certainly sounds like it.

In the same breath the self-satisfied haw-haw, so un-attractive to those of lesser birth, which can be heard in the purlieus of the City, Army and landed sections of the Conservative Party, has given way in society to more reasonable accentuation. But games will be played and new words will become today's flavour, only to be dis-covered by the uninitiated, dropped, and other ones brought into usage. Lady Rothermere, wife of the press baron Vere (*née*) Harmsworth, once explained to me the workings of a language which she had invented. It was a kind of code understood by only a few, and involved the subtraction (or was it addition?) of vowels at predesig-nated points which made a seeming nonsense.

It was an attempt at being different from all those other people out there with whom one has nothing in common. In the same way a casual reader who happens upon *Rolling Stone* magazine, American *Variety* or our own *New Musical Express*, let alone any hi-fi magazine, may think he's entered a world devoid of standard English. Those magazines, you see, are only for the initiated.

The professions are equally guilty of inventing gibber-
ish – the purpose of which is to confuse and conceal so as to
make the job appear difficult. The media, especially news-
papers, television and films, brought in a dozen new
words or at least gave them different meanings. Some
have passed into antiquity – no journalist ever gets on the
blower these days but he does go on *freebies*, comes back and
writes a *puff-par*. The film crew (when not calculating
their expenses, *exes*) are into *noddies*, tracking shots, cut-
aways, talking heads and *fluffs*.

The world has passed Nancy Mitford's U and Non-U
by. Most people know, even if they come from fairly lowly
backgrounds, that it is unwise to ask the way to the toilet,
or to be pleased to meet someone, to ask for the cruet, to sit
on a settee in the lounge or to say pardon when burping.
The socially secure tend to be particularly vulgar and see
no great wrong in ridding themselves of flatulence – as
long as it does not cause undue discomfort/embarrass-
ment to the company.

Psycobabble

A language used by those who have probably visited the
'analyst' and want to impress on the people they meet that
they are concerned about getting-it-together and unfold-
ing the mysteries of the universe. It is also an attempt to
show others that you are not satisfied with 'the terrible-
ness' that surrounds urban man. This ultra-complicated
jargon (which really means nothing) is a way of disguising
what are the fairly ordinary states of man: happiness,
unhappiness, dissatisfaction, fear, the need to be considered unusual – a one-off.

'Sally – I can't come to your party as I've this emotional
black-out at the moment which is compounded by my
diffused awareness.' *Interpretation:* 'I'm feeling emotional

Manic feelings . . .

and would rather be alone – besides, no one would pay attention to my problem.'

'I've got these manic feelings towards you.' *Interp:* 'I sometimes like you and I sometimes hate you.'

'I'm working myself through a weekend fear programme.' *Interp:* 'I have to go to the zoo with Billy and he will want to go to the reptile house – and this I have got to face in order to become a fuller human being.'

'My analyst says that my narcissism is part of the age and so natural.' *Interp:* 'The disorder can be restored through submission or by domination – in this case by the psychiatrist who is keen for you to keep coming for obvious reasons.'

'The encounter group decided I was suffering from stress which explains my negative antagonism towards them.'

Interp: 'While they are all distressed I am filled with a fear of having too much money, too many friends and being too well loved – so this is distress based on euphoria.'

'I have these negative therapeutic reactions which culminate in dehumanizing tendencies.' *Interp:* 'I don't think my analyst is doing me any good and I want to kill him.'

Shrinks like YAVIS – they are the patients they most admire – young, attractive, verbal, intelligent and successful.

Calspeak – *incorporating New York*

dorkiness – everybody is rated by their dorkiness, which is their 'jerk' factor.

ya-da-ya-da-ya-da – replaces blah-blah-blah

humongous – gigantic

pig-out – overeat

it's all about – such as spring or Christmas

get my act together – Americans have been doing this for years

take a hike Mac/why don't you getta outta my face – police talk which could be translated by the London bobby as 'Move along now'

hey man can I share your space? – can I go along with you?

Pub talk

(With thanks to Jeffrey Bernard of the *Spectator*, whose research and practice in this field is undisputed)

how's your better half?
haven't you got 'omes to be going to?
just a swift pint
force one down
are you from this neck of the woods?

a ding-dong (Bells)
tincture
gee and tee (gin and tonic)
long time no see
cheers, squire
I've only got one pair of hands
similar?
don't tell my bank manager
cold enough for you then?
what's your medicine?

Media talk

'In a country which is so conscious of accents it does not surprise me that there have been complaints about mine. I think it is quite legitimate for people not to like my accent – and that it is this dislike which makes them say they cannot understand me.'

Arianna Stassinopoulos – after leaving a BBC TV show

Ripponspeak

This is actually the BBC's pronounciation unit, which is why guerilla comes to you as *gueerilla* and Kabul as *Car bull*.

Gossip-columnese buzzwords

libidinous – oversexed
exotic cheroot – joint
starlet – failed actress, 'hostess'
tired – drunk
constant companion – lover
soi-disant – self-styled upstart
confirmed bachelor – homosexual
willowy – gangly

freeloader on a freebie – hack on a free trip
plug – mention
my good friend Lord X – styled to annoy subject who has
    probably been litigious in the past
Lothario – stud
former beauty – hag
close friendship – affair
City whizz-kid – business sharp
tacky – something in bad taste
pulchritudinous – pretty
exotic – foreign
fun-loving – promiscuous

Film/TV/radio

talking heads
talk-back – from interviewer to producer via headphones
tracking shot
out of camera
jump cut – a bad edit
'all right, take ten' – permission by director to take a ten-
    minute break
action-cut
print it
hair in the gate
good tele
sparks/chippy – electrician and carpenter
punch-up – studio discussion between opposing factions
down the line – interview from studio to studio
cans – headphones

'There's no doubt that the English are the most accent
conscious people in the world.'

Milton Schulman – a Canadian

Anglo-Jewish

this I have got to see

now he tells me
he's a schmuck
he's a meshuggeneh (crazy – as in other drivers)
I'll have to schlepp up to Hampstead for you
all right, already
to a dog it shouldn't happen
. . . of an evening
inside his stomach it should grow a trolley car (example from
    Larry Adler, who says it is an insult used on the streets
    of New York)

Legalese

Barristers

be that as it may or	a good point has been
that's as maybe	made against the barrister, who is anxious to move on to a new point
with all due respect	with no respect
I'm instructed that	and I don't believe it for a minute but a man is entitled to a fair trial
in my submission	I think
it's a matter for you	unfortunately, it's the jury's decision
I'm obliged	thank you
not insignificant	never significant
on the one hand . . . but on the other	hedging bets
within the parameters of the case	perimeters

Judges

your counsel has said all that could possibly be said on your behalf	shut up, he's droned on long enough

79

you may have got the impression
that I hold a particular view of
this case — but you must put that
out of your mind

unless, of course, you
respect my judgement and
agree with me

I hear what you say

but don't expect me to
believe a word of it

Solicitors

unless we hear from you by first
post on Monday our client will
take such steps as he may be
advised

pay up or we'll sue

our client has no wish to
be unreasonable

we've told him he's got no
case

we are in the process of taking
counsel's opinion

we're frantically trying
to find your file

we require your instructions

we haven't got a clue

take counsel's opinion in order to
confirm our view of the matter

and need a barrister to do it
for us

Mr Rumbold is detained
taking instruction just now

no he's not — he is having a
snifter at the Wig and Pen

'I hear what you say' (but don't expect me to believe
a word of it)

The youthful, sporty look is now what everybody,
darling, is wearing

10

Fashion

'Never despise fashion, it's what we have instead of a god.'

Malcolm Bradbury

The revelation that the Duke of Kent, who is vice-chairman of the British Overseas Trade Board, had some suits made for him in Hong Kong indicates that most sensible people are turning away from the prices now being charged in Savile Row. The Duke's decision to have some suiting made up in the colony caused a predictable outburst by several Labour MPs – notably Bob Cryer, who probably buys his suits at Marks & Spencer. It was, he screamed, 'a disgrace that he (the Duke) should even contemplate such a savage act of disloyalty'.

It then came to light that Princess Margaret, Princess Anne and the Queen all had clothes made for them in Honkers by Mr M. S. Soong's bespoke firm Soong Salon De Mode. He said Princess Anne bought five dresses during a visit in 1971 and the Queen had a skirt, a cocktail dress, an evening gown and topcoat run up for her.

All except the very rich are now eschewing the outrageously expensive *haute couture* houses – who anyway seem to design for the more mature woman.

The youthful sporty look is now what everybody, darling, is wearing. It consists of T-shirts, linen trousers, loose jackets, striped blazers, flat shoes, and is interchangeable between men and women. In America this is called the 'preppy' look and, because our fashion gurus cannot think of a better phrase, it is one being bandied arounded the London *salons*. The ethnic look of the late sixties is OUT-OUT (the stuff you picked up on your trek to Katmandu – the cheesecloth skirts, espadrilles and the like – should be dumped), and its place has been taken by a fresher, neater, outdoor look. Suntans, be they obtained by hours on a sun bed or out of a bottle, are a necessary accoutrement to this look. There is a new mood of precision about and there is no longer the need to bedeck oneself in accessories.

Men should attempt to be boyish and sporty – not difficult for anyone who has been to a public school – as the scarf and blazer look is with us.

While it has never been wrong to patronize the workmanship of Savile Row, where a suit can cost in excess of £450, the more frugally minded toff has been searching out moonlighting tailors from the established firms. If you can bear to live without a label which says 'Huntsman' or 'Blades' then the suit run up on the quiet is for you.

There are dangers in the path of the man who is out to impress by his choice of clothes. Remember, while gentlemen almost always have clean shoes, they can frequently be seen in shirts which have seen better days.

A former colleague used to turn up to the office with impeccably starched white linen or striped shirts, with silk Hermes ties to match, and his choice of double-breasted tailored suits was the envy of the fashion-page writers. The effect was complete with his highly polished Gucci loafers and perfectly coiffured blond hair. Another colleague, who prided himself on wearing his grandfather's hunting raincoat and, believe it or not, a couple of his pre-war suits, used to look down in amazement at this tailor's dummy. One lunchtime he could not resist remarking in the direction of this over-elegant figure, and fingering a frayed lapel, he said: 'Dear boy – you're almost too well dressed to be a gentleman!' The resultant destruction of the peacock said everything.

Where fashion is headed no one knows. But it seems the

recent impetus and inspiration has come from the punk movement – which is right out of working-class culture. It was the kids who gathered on King's Road who started the worldwide craze for dressing anarchically. It will be they – and not the designers listed below – who are responsible for the return of the miniskirt and for the return of two-tone (black and white).

'I think by the end of the month men will be wearing powdered wigs, white face make-up and cosmetics on their hands – and women will be into bustles.'

Steve Strange, founder of the Electro-Disko

Tailors

IN	OUT
Vincent	Gieves & Hawkes
Blades	Nutter's
Hawes & Curtis	Harrods
Kilgour, French and Stanbury and Bernard Weatherill (I hope they don't put all that on the label)	
H. Huntsman (suits start at £660 and DJs at £854)	
W. G. Child of Wandsworth High St	
Henry Poole	
Cyril Castle	
Davies & Son (old peerage)	

Women's shoe shops and designers

IN	OUT
Clive Shilton (for his Zig and Zag range)	Midas
	Rayne
Ferragamo	Gucci
Manolo Blahnik	Elliot
Ryder	K Shoes
Katrina	Ravel
Berties	Russell and Bromley
Kurt Geiger	Lilley and Skinner
Buno Magli	Medway
Zapata	Pambos and Claude
Guido Pasquali	Terry de Havilland
Charles Jourdan	
Roland Cartier	

Men's shoe shops and makers

IN	OUT
Lobb's	Bally
Henry Maxwell at Huntsman	Gucci
Alan McAfee	Russell and Bromley and all other chains
Fosters	
Tricker's	
Wildsmith	
Lloyd Jennings	
Poulsen, Skone & Co.	

Shirt makers

IN	OUT
Bowring Arundel	James Drew
Turnbull and Asser	Hilditch and Key
Harvie and Hudson	Sulka
Budd	T & A look-alikes from Hong Kong
Coles	
New and Lingwood	Monogrammed shirts
Deborah and Clare	All shirts with matching ties

Designers

IN	OUT
Jean Muir	Dior (and all *haute couture*)
Jasper Conran	Yuki
Roland Klein	Ossie Clark
Strawberry Studios	Thea Porter
Katherine Hamnet	Adrian Cartmell
Maxfield Parrish	Anthony Ma
Zandra Rhodes	John Bates
Claude Montana	Bill Gibb
Jean Paul Gaultier	Jean Varon
Kalvin Klein	Janice Wainwright
Norma Kamali	(popular in USA)
Tom Bell (must for ball gowns)	Halston
Thierry Mugler	Hartnell
Nineva Khomo	

'The perfect woman must be haughty but not too beautiful . . . she must be a slave to her clothes and jewels.'

Salvador Dali

11

The Dinner Party

'I stick to cold things in the summer – like gull's eggs and cold salmon.'

Nigel Dempster

The dinner party is the highest form of entertainment, when guests are on their mettle and prepared to sing for their supper. The hostess must strive for a certain homogeneity in her guests – it's no good putting scientific minded people alongside a bunch of Bohemian artists. But this is not to say all the participants should have the same outlook on life – that would result in torpor. Indeed, it is better if guests know each other as they feel freer to take up a combatant role and to be rude to other guests. This banter is what dinner parties are all about and it is up to the hostess to foster the atmosphere to induce coruscating conversation.

To these ends guests should be kept topped up with wine (*in vino veritas*) which can be drunk without fear of the source drying up. If it does, your reputation as a hostess will be at stake and you will quickly earn a name for frugality. The ideal number of guests for a dinner party has been put at six, but that is not to say a much larger gathering cannot be fun. Barbara Cartland has said of her daughter the Countess Spencer that her interpretation of a little dinner party is two dozen people sitting around with all the women in tiaras. It is nice to know that this is still going on at Althorp, but I fear such style is beyond the reach of most of us.

Gone are the days when no comment was passed on the food, as you can never be sure that the hostess has not had a hand in its creation. As always you would expect the food to be of an excellence but no harm can be done by complimenting the provider – by that I don't mean Grace should be said ... although it should if you have a senior churchman along.

It is still considered rather bad form to attempt all the cooking personally – unless you can convince the guests that the help has gone off at short notice. This is not a persuasive excuse, as you could have hired a cook for the day. In fact to do (or supervise) the cooking for a DP is not as looked down upon as it once was – on the condition that you are not constantly darting off to the kitchen to ensure the *soufflé* has not collapsed or the *hollandaise* separated. The guests will want to see you in a happy frame of mind – not in a terrible tizz because the cream-of-watercress soup has curdled or the salmon has been guzzled by the cat.

Tessa Kennedy, a renowned hostess, insists on getting the right mix of people, selects food in the *nouvelle cuisine* style, and gets someone else to cook it. The British no longer give very lavish dinner parties like the French or Americans – who are quite capable of spending thousands recreating an underwater scene or 'a heavenly effect' with clouds billowing over the guests and empyrean music playing gently in the background. Stavros Niarchos is reputed to have given a large-scale dinner party last year when he built a ballroom with glass walls and made the scene look like a Normandy garden by sticking real apple trees in the middle of all the tables. This is perhaps going too far, although one French noble gave a party in which a beautiful maiden – in fact, the host's lover – was borne down a graceful flight of stairs on a bed carried by semi-naked 'slave girls' who were painted in gold and lighted by bewigged footmen holding candles. This is a long way from having six friends around the pine kitchen table with French onion soup for starters, lasagne to follow and *crème brulée* for pudding.

The lack of money does not exclude a resourceful hostess from putting on an elegant show or inventing a clever idea such as throwing an all-red party. This can be taken to extremes (I was once forced to eat blue potato in which a salmon was swimming), and guests will have to struggle through things made out of red cabbage, beetroot, red beans, carrots, tomatoes, redcurrants and rhubarb. Whatever – it is the hostess's duty to create an ambience in which her guests will feel pampered and indulged and in this way the most revealing behaviour will emerge. After all, reputations either as a wit, bore, raconteur, vulgarian, intellect or conversationalist are made or lost at the slippery area which is a good dinner party.

'You need a good cook, a good cast, and good wine. And none of that is any good at all without a good hostess.'

Roger Moore (007)

Food

IN	OUT
roast beef, lamb	steaks, particularly well done
all game during the season	
steak and kidney pie with oysters	avocado and prawns
	roast chicken
York ham	beef olives
fresh salmon, smoked salmon with scrambled eggs	most *quiches* (fine for picnics)
	most *soufflés* (overdone)
trout	chili con carne (for supper parties)
most fish – especially bream, bass, brill and sole	kipper or mackerel *pâté*
most seafoods except scampi and squid	garlic bread
	baked grapefruit

90

'Taramasalata — well, he is Greek, darling'

authentic curry (only if
made by old colonials)
moules marinières
watercress soup
pea and ham soup
nettle soup
blini with caviar
charcuterie
almost all salads
intelligent use of all herbs
summer pudding
bread and butter pudding
(snack parties)
melon and *prosciutto* ham
globe artichokes
asparagus
fish soup with *rouille* (one
dish where lots of garlic is
permissible)
crudités
syllabub
home-made ice cream
fruit salad
spotted dick (you would be
surprised how many peers
remember it from the
nursery and love it – c.f.
House of Lords dining
room menu)
devils on horseback
angels on horseback
gulls' eggs

hot avocado
all health foods; organic
cheese, veg, yoghurt,
coffee, etc.
tournedos en croûte – for that
matter everything else *en
croûte*
margarine
chicken coronation
cheesecake
crêpes suzette (far too flashy)
lobster thermidor
duck *à l'orange*
crème brulée (bachelor's
standby)
spag. bol.
French onion soup
ratatouille
taramasalata and pitta
bread
turkey escalopes *cordon bleu*
veal – for moral reasons
cheese dips
paella
stuffed peppers
-ini food – *fettuccine,
fagiolini, tagliarini,
zucchine*, etc.

Table furniture

IN	OUT
individual salt cellar and pepper mills	wine coolers
candles/candlesticks	silver-like ornaments such as pheasants and horses
flowers	fish knives (a middle-class nicety)
menus for grand occasions	
cut glass	wine baskets
linen napkins	napkin rings (implies you are going to use them again)
silver-crested base platter for the very special DP	
finger bowls (as above – but do not put them out when entertaining foreigners, as they are prone to drink from them)	oven to table ware (unless in the country)
	placement (place cards are rather pompous, as you should know in your head where you want your guests to sit)
soup spoons (the English version looks like a large desert spoon)	
Minton, Crown Derby or, better, Wedgwood china	table mats (unless a hot plate is going to ruin your French polish)
fruit pyramids	more than three glasses at each setting (you're not giving a state banquet)

Restaurants

'Restaurants are much too expensive. I only go once in a while just to prove I am not stingy.'

Viscount Weymouth

IN	OUT
Le Gavroche	Drones
L'Escapade (especially for cocktails)	La Brasserie
	San Lorenzo
Langan's Brasserie	San Frediano
Eleven Park Walk	San Rufillo
Savoy Restaurant (not Grill)	À l'Écu de France
The Ritz	Bill Bentley's
Connaught Hotel Restaurant	Claridge's Restaurant
	Hungry Horse
Tante Claire	Lacy's
Bewicks	Lockets
Khans	Quaglino's Restaurant
La Famiglia	Rules
Standard Indian	Shezan
Holy Cow	Veeraswamy's
White Tower	Wiltons
Carrier's	Cecconi's
Interlude	Ochio Rios Room
Le Chef	Bistro Vino
Golden Duck	The Colony
Leith's	Il Girasole
Ma Cuisine	Joe Allen's
Manzi's	La Poule au Pot
Meridiana	I Paparazzi
Mirabelle	Alexander's
Parkes	Chez Nico
Poons (Lisle Street)	Friends
Le Poulbot	Kundan

Scott's

Thomas de Quincey

Vendome

Marie Claire

Gay Hussar

The English House

Waltons

Brinkley's

Le Caspia

Overton's

Poissonnerie de l'Avenue

Sheekey's

Le Suquet

Julie's

Mon Plaisir

Tai-Pan

Bianchi's

Bertorelli's

Mr Kai of Mayfair

Porters

Mr Chow

Hard Rock

Ivy

Kettner's

Langan's Bistro

Tiberio

Étoile

12

The INs & OUTs of Social Mobility

'History teaches us that, however imperfect our systems are, they have not prevented many men of modest origins rising to the top.'

Lord 'RAB' Butler

One of the classic ways of social enhancement is through occupation and association. Any job which brings the socially ambitious within reach of a set of people who mix in more exalted circles will enhance his or her chances of infiltration.

The Nuffield Social Mobility Survey, carried out by sociologists under the direction of (the upwardly mobile?) Professor Halsey and Dr John Goldthorpe, is grim reading for the working-class kid trying to make his way in life.

But raging social ambition, rather than the wish for job improvement, is generally found within the ranks of the lower middle classes, whose women will stop at nothing to advance the career and status of their husbands. For them this survey is light at the end of the tunnel.

The sociologists questioned more than 10,000 men in 1972 and found that there had been considerable upward social mobility from this rank, with more people reaching the top because of the general economic progress and changes in occupational structure. But they concluded that there had been no change at all in the relative chances of reaching the top of those born into other social classes.

They discovered, of course, that the inequalities of educational opportunity had persisted – as will always be true while the increasingly expensive public school system exists and along with it the human desire of people to 'better' themselves and their children. Yet the mobility study showed that British society was remarkably open in the twentieth century. Far from being an exclusive élite caste the service class (barristers, managers, administrators and some City businessmen) have recruited widely from those of other social backgrounds. (Is this because there are not enough public schoolboys to go around?) As a result, they claim, it has become a class of low classness, heterogeneous and without any clear sense of identity. That is not strictly true – as any foreign visitor who happens upon a City watering hole at lunchtime will agree. Before him he would see a mass of pinstripe suits, brogues, briefcases and waves of wha-wha rising with the smoke.

In reality social mobility has never been difficult in Britain because in the long run success in this field is based

Pinstripe suits and waves of wha-wha .

on money. In the short term the acquisition of money is hugely despised, mainly because the *nouveaux-riches* are so inept at spending their new-gotten gains with any degree of taste. This arouses loathing and envy in the class above them who have made the successful transition from the mediocre level to a more elevated one – again thanks in the most part to the accumulation of wealth. Unlike the system in the Indian subcontinent where, like it or not, you are stuck with the caste into which you are born, our system is much less rigid.

In India there is no movement within social layers, because if you are unfortunately born into the bottom-level fisher caste, for the luckless reason that centuries ago someone determined that fishing is what your family were assigned to do, a fisherman is what you remain. This does not mean you have to earn your living by casting nets as indeed you can go on to make a fortune as a property magnate or hotel-chain owner. But financial success counts for not a fig under the caste system. The property magnate will not be permitted to enter the mud house of a brahmin, who although he may be living in relative poverty, belongs to the high caste. It must be death for social climbers.

In this country the first-generation successful merchant can achieve 'gentry' status for his family in about two or three generations, although he can never aspire to elevate the family into the aristocracy, whose ranks are virtually sealed.

The path of upward mobility is well established. The children are sent off to prep and public school where by osmosis they go up a peg. They will be encouraged to mix with 'people who matter' and to cultivate suitable friends. A service profession will be obligatory and marriage into an 'old', if not particularly well-off, family will complete the circle. As long as the accumulation of wealth is kept at a constant flow the succeeding generations will go through the same process. A decent family house will be obtained and with it a useful parcel of land. Within a few decades the gentrification procedure will have been achieved and a new member of the upper classes has come into being.

A useful example of upward mobility rests with the Prime Minister, who has become a member, nay a bastion, of the upper reaches of the middle class. It is ironical that through political expediency it was necessary for her and her aides to point out that she was born in very 'ordinary' circumstances and was, I believe, brought up above a grocer's shop in Grantham. Mrs Thatcher would argue in favour of a meritocracy and in part she has got to the top through her undoubted intelligence and ability. And yet she still needed the approbation of the Tory diehards in order to advance up the party ladder. A meritocrat she no doubt is, but still her cabinet consists of about sixty per cent public school chaps, and Old Etonians are more than well represented. Her Foreign Secretary is a peer and many of her senior colleagues are landed gentlemen (Pym, Whitelaw, Gilmour, Hailsham) and do not fit into the new Conservative mould at all. Mrs T.'s grandchildren will, I suggest, be firmly entrenched members of the upper middle classes and with some luck will have the then Dame Thatcher of Lamberhurst (or wherever) around to thank for their rapid climb from humble beginnings to the dizzy social heights.

If the present holder of the exalted post of First Lord of the Admiralty decides to reintroduce hereditary peerages, as has been suggested she will, there will be an almost imperceptible scramble for a real title – so much more valuable than a life peerage. Such an act would once again open up the lower ranks of the aristocracy – although new title-holders will be regarded as parvenu peers for quite a while. It is bound to cause angry grumbles from the opposition benches, and Mrs T. will have added fuel to the class war which smoulders away beneath the fabric of modern-day society just as it has done for generations.

So you think you are smart!

You ARE if you can
* trace your line back to William the Conqueror
* claim to have lived in the same house for around four centuries
* claim to have a family church filled with family hatchments
* claim to a title which goes back to Tudor times or before
* muster together a decent array of quartering on your coat of arms
* claim kinship with Nell Gwynn, Macbeth, John of Gaunt or Nelson
* prove that you are related to the Queen
* point to a London village which is synonymous with your name
* claim your work is running the estate, which should be 4,000 acres plus

But you are NOT if you
* insist tradesmen call you by your courtesy title
* get your secretary to phone *The Times* because your birthday is approaching and they might like to record this fact
* hire a butler for the night
* have a junior title (Ypres, Monckton, Montgomery, Edinburgh)
* sneak along to the College of Heralds to acquire armorial bearings
* insist on renewing your entry to *Burke's Landed*

Gentry when you have been reduced to a two-bed semi in Eastbourne

* put your sons down for Eton on birth because it is the thing to do

* become the self-appointed squire of a village and take it upon yourself to restore the local church in order to acquire status

* have made a fortune in the last century, be it through coal, manufacture of soap, or exploitation of natives in the Commonwealth countries

13

Sex, Manners and Marriage

'What's a promiscuous person? It's usually someone who is having more sex than you are.'

Victor Lownes

Upper-class attitudes to sex differ from those of the middle and lower – although there is increasing collusion in this field. Actually to have 'an attitude' towards sex is considered more than a little old fashioned as almost everyone is doing it. While the traditional values are being eroded almost as quickly as an ice sculpture in a sticky ballroom there are some rules which must not be broken. It is still a cad and a bounder who talks about his sexual conquests; and if it gets around that you are a sexual braggart you will be treated with the utmost distrust by members of the opposite sex.

Sexual *mores* are usually formed at school, which is just as well because the children of the upper class suffer from their parents' all-consuming embarrassment in telling them about the facts of life. It is just assumed that what they have not picked up watching the horses, dogs and bulls at home they will learn at boarding school.

The middles, ever conscious that their teenage daughter could let the side down by getting pregnant out of marriage, attempt to explain, usually from an ignorant/innocent point of view, the mysteries of sex education.

The more down-to-earth working class, who suffer from a fierce pride and in many cases a low-church morality, expect their sons to be a bit wayward and their daughters to be virtuous. Like the uppers they never discuss sex at home and rely on the state education system to provide the answers.

In the same way, the upper crust expect the biology master to explain all to their offspring – even if the lesson is disguised by taking the sexually prolific rabbit as an example.

All this can have disastrous effects, although it is being too simplistic to subcribe to the view that all ex-public schoolboys are sexual and emotional cripples. One prep-school headmaster did brave his natural reticence by calling in all those boys who were approaching, or wrestling with, raging puberty. If any of the boys got the urge – almost everyone did at some stage in the night – they were implored to take a walk or better still have a brisk cold shower. The 'don't-touch-it' syndrome was still prevalent but the advice imparted by the headmaster could not have been more impracticable. Being housed in a historic manor which was named in the Domesday Book, anyone attempting a nocturnal stroll along those ancient and creaking corridors would have needed an unshakable faith in the Almighty or nerves of tungsten.

Being deprived of female company for such a vital part of their lives (sexually speaking, men reach their zenith at 18 – women at 30) inevitably leaves its mark. The just-out-of-schools tend to be sexually immature – their comprehensive school counterparts have done it all by the time they are 18 – which has the effect of turning them into dreadful macho-man studs. All they think about is the pursuit and they lap up girls rather like a thirsty blood-hound at a bowl of water.

The sexually awkward stage is one when deep resentment of parents sets in, but the mood goes fairly quickly – as soon as the gaucherie vanishes with experience. With the admission of girls to public schools the complexion has changed; there is now more room for experimentation.

If most of these comments are restricted to the male

party it is because girls have fewer problems than their male counterparts at school; their role, at this stage, is a more passive one.

Kissing, etc.

If the traditional manners are being eroded, genuine old-fashioned courtesy is still appreciated. No one these days worries about which way the port is passed or if medals are to be worn, except for a few rich Greek boys who are thrown into confusion when they try to enter English society. The general decay of the 'manners makyth man' attitude has come about through the actions of the women's liberation movement, which has done a grave disservice to womanhood by promoting the canard that women are equal to men. As any athlete knows, this is not the case and most female females are happy with the difference. The sisters of the hairy-leg brigade (by the way, what is it they have got against personal hygiene?) have made it harder for men to act in a mannered way towards women. Yet there has been a strong reaction to the grey utilitarian age in which we live – and that is the birth of punk. At the other end of the scale there is a noticeable flamboyance, if not in matters of dress, in manners. While it is no longer necessary to leap from your seat at a restaurant table every time a woman returns or to open a car door when disembarking, it is important to show that you know it is correct to doff your hat at the approach of a lady.

Good manners are taught to the well-bred almost from birth (it is amazing that infants are not saying please and thank you at the breast), while the working class find it very difficult to say thank you. This is not out of lack of politeness but out of awkwardness – so the very display of good manners indicates that you are of some breeding. Kissing is an upper-class pastime which in recent years has become almost obligatory.

A full-blooded sloppy . . .

While the handshake lingers on, and has its place when greeting the vicar after matins or at the more stuffy diplomatic function, the more than perfunctory kiss is now a must. Social kissing must be done with conviction or the act will appear to be noncommital and thus throw the recipient of your greeting into confusion. The disastrous effect will be of two feigning heads bobbing towards and away from each other without making contact. Most women expect to be pecked once on both cheeks and it is safest to stick to that system, but some sophisticates go for a full-blooded sloppy on the lips. This can be fun if the female (or male) party is not wearing too heavy a layer of lipstick – which is a devil to get off and ruins the taste of wine.

The other form of kissing which can be employed quite successfully to strangers and dowagers is the kiss to the hand. It has made something of a comeback since our membership to the EEC (well, that is my theory), but such foppishness does not really suit the more dignified nature of the Anglo-Saxon. Incidentally, it is this nature which gets in the way of most Englishmen on the dance floor – they resemble crazed insects as they shake their limbs around in a decisively uncoordinated fashion. It is even more important to carry out this difficult manoeuvre with positiveness or again it will end in disaster. The bemused lady who you are trying to impress will wonder what you are doing as you make a half-hearted plunge for her hand. She will probably get the impression that you are after her bag and call for assistance. Much skill is needed in the execution if this is not to happen, so the unconfident should leave it alone and settle for the afore-mentioned facial peck.

It is also inadvisable to try kissing the hand of someone with feminist sympathies, as such a person will almost certainly disapprove and regard the whole performance as pretentious and condescending.

'Kissing has become almost *de rigueur* when greeting friends and even acquaintances.'

Charlotte Ford in her Book of Modern Manners

Weddings

IN	OUT
to announce forthcoming marriage in *The Times*	to announce forthcoming marriage in the *Daily Telegraph*
to avoid it before 30 (like Prince Charles) for men;	to elope to Gretna Green

to avoid it before 24 – for women

to have masses of clergy officiating – a bishop on hand is a plus

to get married in a country church

for brides to wear a lace veil which has been in the family for generations

to put out invitations which are engraved and measure 5½ inches by 7 inches

to have a toastmaster

to serve good champagne and short-eats

to hold receptions in a marquee in the garden of the bride's family

to sabotage the couple's car with kippers on the manifold, etc.

to have a party afterwards for the guests

to follow the example of Romeo and Juliet

to marry in a register office – if it is the first time

to have tunnels of anything (hose pipes, folk dancers' sticks, flags, javelins, etc.), except swords for Army officers

to put out invitations which remind guests that morning-dress will be worn

to have a best man who tells vulgar jokes

to have a sit-down do at which sausage rolls and veal and ham pie are served

to serve sherry and Asti Spumante

to have a reception in the village/town hall

to have too much bunting on the hired Rolls-Royce

to throw confetti with silver horseshoes in it

Married life

DO

have a vasectomy – but who will believe you?

ask for your fiancée's hand in marriage – shows you have courtesy and will

DON'T

brag about conquests – this goes for women too

smoke in bed

take coffee with him after he's given you dinner, if

enhance chances of better present from prospective in-laws

flirt madly because it is what society is all about

have liaisons but be discreet

arrive – like Army officers do

live together before marriage

take baths and showers together – saves water

you don't want an away fixture

be illegal

champion the cause of gay lib – it's old hat and will exclude you from certain clubs/*salons*, etc.

become a sexual neurotic over performance

undress in the same room as your partner – preserve some mystery

attempt to make love when drunk

go to wife-swopping parties – terribly *News of the World*

resort to sex-manuals or follow the lead of Molly Parkin heroines

brag that you have slept with Martin Amis, Dai Llewellyn, Lord Weymouth

stuff a colleague – sound advice from the late, great Nicholas Tomalin

Love tokens
Her to him

IN	OUT
An Omega quartz 1355 watch – thinner than an After Eight mint at 1.48 mm – just £4,500	A box of his favourite cigars – it will make kissing rather nasty
	A set of monogrammed

A peacock to put in his garden (it will scream in the mating season and thus keep you in mind)

An ounce of Bijan men's perfume at £200, obtainable from LA

The use of Daddy's yacht when Daddy is away

500 grams of Sevruga

A side of Scotch smoked salmon

Your portrait by Haliday

A bunch of flowers – it's not the male prerogative to give them

A new bow-tie because you can't stand his old one

A case of champagne (see list)

A case of Château Latour 70

A cigarette holder – this is a subtle hint that you disapprove of the habit

A leather bound copy of *Debrett's Peerage and Baronetage* – if he features

Gold money-clip

A dozen golf balls with his name on them – and a golf ball finder set

A surprise party

A lock of your hair in suitable locket

A set of Irish linen sheets

handkerchiefs

A briefcase

A year's subscription to the *Horse and Hound*

Socks

An old school/regimental tie

A bowler from Lock's

Underwear

Pens

Personalized number-plate

A Sodastream

A wine atlas

A Fabergé-like egg

Ginseng

A desk set

A paperweight

Monogrammed slippers

A monogrammed shirt

Case of Muscadet

'Silver' tankard

Ship's decanter

Pearl shirt studs

Tin cufflinks – silver/gold will do

Wallets

Cash

A home-made cake in the shape of a heart

A personal message in *The Times*

The Joy of Sex or other such manual

T-shirts

Red roses

Boxed record set of his
favourite opera plus
tickets to the real thing
A Hesketh superbike

Him to her

IN	OUT
An IATA travel card to enable her to fly on your account	A Slendertone machine
	A replica of your signet ring
	A selection of hand soaps
A biorhythm machine	A ticket for a QE2 cruise
A mink	Hang-gliding lessons
A rose bush	Cookery lessons
A neon sculpture	A portrait of yourself
A Black Lab puppy	A steam iron
A Harrods' hamper full of out-of-season food	A lock of your hair in a locket
A David Shilling hat	A selection of Tupperware
A hunter	A pinball machine
Keys to your flat	A sun lamp
Something from Janet Reger	A cube of gold/platinum
A selection of Thomas Hardy love-poems signed by the author	A ship's decanter
	A red rose
	A corn dolly
A season ticket to the opera	A monogrammed cut glass
A Ceylon sapphire	A Tiffany lamp
The use of your driver	A singing telegram to
A George III teapot	convey your love
The dedication of your first novel to her	Pearls – they can be taken to mean tears
A silk jump-suit by Arte	A pair of roller skates
A quill pen	A Nicholas Treadwell
Wimbledon Final ticket	'dummy'
An Etienne Aigner vanity case	A Magimix
A personalized T-shirt	A cassette of you warbling your favourite song

110

14

The Garden

Gardening has a fascination for both rich and poor and it is a peculiarly English obsession not practised with much enthusiasm by Greeks, Germans or the French, who were responsible for the tedious formal garden. In contrast the country cottage garden with its snapdragons, hollyhocks, climbing roses and hardy annuals is the embodiment of all things English.

On a larger scale the nobility have always spent money laying out gardens with water terraces, sculptured hedges, fountains and mazes. There was considerable snob appeal in propagating exotic fruits from the East and in creating fruits like the greengage.

No country house is complete without a walled garden, hedge mazes, grass pathways, greenhouses which contain mysterious vegetables and fruits frequently protected and ruled over by a tyrannical head gardener who forbids entry even to members of the household.

Today the garden is yet another area where one's taste and discernment are on the line. The subtle clues one can pick up of a family's standing by walking through their house can be further reinforced by a stroll in their garden.

Although there are many grander, the garden at the Sitwells' Derbyshire house Renishaw Hall is imbued with indelible aristocratic flavour. Evelyn Waugh once stood with the hall's former owner, Sir George Sitwell, and was captivated by the view of the valley below with its farms, cottages, railway and colliery. One can easily summon up the imagination and see Dame Edith, the old literary battleaxe, and her brothers walking Indian file in silence, through the garden.

Ruled over by a tyrannical head gardener

Most houses can no longer keep a full-time garden staff (or outside staff, as they used to be known) and most owners of large houses spend the summer months mowing their lawns. One Yorkshire landowner once calculated that he walked about ten miles every time he brought out the Suffolk Punch. (That's not a horse, more of a lawn-mower.) It kept him fit for the shooting season and kept his mind off the state of the country and what the unions were doing to it.

On a smaller scale it is difficult to say why the nasty nasturtium has no place in a gentleman's garden, unless it is planted to cover a rubbish tip, or why hydrangeas fed on a diet of rusty razorblades are generally unacceptable – whereas the rhododendron is splendidly aristocratic. A plastic pond in which goldfish are deposited is common, while a natural lily pond or lake is tasteful and pleasing to the eye.

In the same way, a statue which leads the eye to the horizon along an avenue of lime trees in a garden on the grand scale gives one an aesthetic experience. But the same thing attempted in a plot of no more than four acres is pretentious and ridiculous. It is the difference between the public park, where the impersonal hand of a city department has been at work, and a garden like Nymans in Sussex (owned by the Countess of Rosse) where creativity and taste has produced a magical gem.

IN

summerhouses
natural lily ponds
rose trellis
outhouses full of garden
    machinery and strings of
    onions
greenhouses ruled over by
    grumpy gardeners and
    containing old vines
bee hives
paths of Portland stone or
    grass
bird baths and rustic
    bird tables
nesting boxes
ivy-clad houses
cottage gardens
swimming pools out of sight
    of the house and of
    irregular shape
hedges
some swing-seats and
    umbrellas
tree houses for children

OUT

do-it-yourself ponds
trees such as the bay in pots
garden 'sculpture' made
    out of concrete
fake wells
crazy paving
topiary (unless on the scale
    of Powis Castle)
street lamps in the garden
wrought-iron gates, seats,
    or any other furniture
built-in barbecues
rockeries, as suburban as
    flowering cherry trees
    and laburnums
gnomes – anyone with
    them must be finding
    this book a puzzle; burn
    them
putting greens

herbaceous borders
terraces
bonfires

Common or garden?
Plants

IN	OUT
Hollyhock	Begonia
Chamomile	Pot marigold
Columbine	Wallflower
Cornflower (excellent Ascot buttonholes)	Chrysanthemum
Clematis	Hyacinth
Nasturtium	Californian poppy
Sweet pea	Fuchsia
Foxglove	Everlasting flower
Snowdrop (snob value in claiming the first out)	Lobelia
Golden rayed lily	Stock
Grape hyacinth	Forget-me-not
Polyanthus	Tobacco plant
Zinnia	Joy weed (not marijuana but a half-hardy annual)
Peony (in country)	Hydrangea
Most roses	Spring bulbs planted in pots
Rhododendrons	Lavender (in town)
Magnolia	Flowering cherry (the expression of suburbia)
Spring bulbs planted at random	
Lupin (in town)	

House plants

IN	OUT
Japonica	Christmas cactus
Begonia rex	Monstera deliciosa
Caladium hybrid	Geranium

114

Azalea (outside only)

Cyclamen

Amaryllis (a vulgar flower)

Miniature trees

Hanging ferns

Cineraria

Gloxinia

Poinsettia

All cacti

Gardens in bottles

Rubber plants

Vegetables to grow

IN	OUT
Globe artichokes	Beetroot
Asparagus	Brussels sprouts
Haricots verts	Cauliflower
Cabbage (white and red)	Chicory
Carrots	Onions (shallots are IN)
Courgettes	Peas (remember not to give
Leeks	them to Princess Anne)
Mushrooms	Parsnip
Mange tout	Marrow
Capsicum (peppers)	Swede
Potatoes (new)	Sea kale beet
Spinach	Turnip
Tomatoes	Mustard and cress
Cucumbers	
Purple broccoli	
Sweet corn	
Pumpkin	
All herbs (no garden is complete without a bed)	
Horseradish	
Garlic	

Fruits to grow

IN	OUT
Crab apple	Apples
English peach	Rhubarb
Pears	Gooseberries

Apricot
Grapes
Cherry
Greengage (invented by
 Lord Gage)
Raspberry
Blackberry
Strawberry
Black and redcurrant
Blueberry

15

Sporting Etiquette

Shooting

Correct behaviour is admired, nay demanded, here more than anywhere else because the general aim is to kill pheasants rather than the guests. People who lack gun sense should not be allowed within range and preferably kept away from human life on shoots. A great deal of value is placed upon an invitation to shoot at a well-stocked estate, as the privilege could cost an outsider around £500 per day on a top grouse moor. Your ability to kill birds will be on display and it will be noted by the host just how well you are doing. It is bad form to keep on missing, as the terrified pheasant which has been fortunate enough to escape with its life might fly to safer habitats – and that could mean the next-door estate.

The way in which you shoot does not matter as long as you are an effective marksman. One of the more curious sights in sporting circles is Lord Lambton – he owns some magnificent shooting in County Durham and Northumberland – who is inclined to pot away while reclining in a deck chair. This unusual habit does not seem to affect his accuracy and he is regarded as one of the finest shots in the country. It is possible to get away with just about anything as long as you are good at what you do.

So it is quite legitimate to 'poach' a bird from a neighbouring butt as long as you can be certain of killing it and administer a cheeky *coup de grâce* by dropping the bird at his feet. Although this demonstrates that you are an ace shot it is unwise to do this once too often in the direction of your host or visiting Royalty. Your next invitation might be a long time coming. Sartorial standards are still main

. . . Pot away while reclining in a deck chair

tained on the smarter shoots and it is advisable to remain traditional in matters of dress. Mr David Hicks, the interior designer and son-in-law of the late Earl Mountbatten of Burma, reputedly once caused a stir by turning up for a day's shooting attired in bright orange check tweeds, floral purple shirt with matching tie and knee-high white sealskin boots.

DO

not be ashamed of bringing along a Spanish gun (who wants to risk damaging a Purdey which is now regarded as an investment?)

wear a husky, green hunters or hand-made leather boots and tailored plus-twos

poach from a neighbour but take care to kill the bird and not him

be certain to tip the head keeper at least £5 if it has been a satisfactory day

offer around your Kings Ginger Liquor which has been known to put the twinkle back into old men's eyes

praise your host or providing so many epic birds – they are the ones which fly fast and high

ensure that your gun is in

DON'T

bring along an over-under, as they are regarded as very bad form and unsporting

wear anything too colourful which will draw attention to yourself

bring along a shooting stick if you wish to be considered young

complain that you have been given a rotten position – if your shooting is off you'll be thankful

use plastic cartridges, as they are considered ecologically unsound because they don't rot

bring along badly behaved dogs, as they are quite liable to get shot by mistake. Labradors are best for open country and spaniels (cocker,

good order and that you
are licensed
give half the bet on the bag to
the Game Conservancy

springer) for thick cover
ever ask your host how
many birds he lays
down, if you have had a
poor day he will be
shamed to admit it was a
great number
be rude to keepers/loaders
swing through the line
commit the cardinal sin of
shooting a hen on a
cocks-only day
carry your gun broken over
your shoulder

Fishing

It is no cliché that the proponents of this sport are the
biggest fibbers around. That is because if you are foolish
enough to spend countless hours up to your waist in a
fast-flowing arctic stream with midges biting chunks out
of your head you must pretend to have got something out
of it. The trouble is on a bad day when the trout/salmon
have not been biting and you have nothing to show for it
people will think you are pretty stupid if you cannot at
least bring back a tale (*sic*) which will make it seem like a
worthwhile experience. Fishermen pay fortunes for this
seeming discomfort and the only thing which keeps them
returning to the rivers is the expectation of catching a
monster on a fly which they have invented. This is fame –
and all the more so if you get your fish stuffed and on
display.

Being purists, all fishermen eschew the use of worms as
bait to catch a salmon although this is by far the most
successful way. They also have scant respect for more
scientific methods of catching fish – nets and dynamite, for

instance. Most owners of decent stretches have a regard for the skill of a poacher if he does not play too dirty. The former Prime Minister, Lord Home of the Hirsel, suffered from a most cheeky poacher who pinched salmon, not from the river, but from the larder.

The etiquette on the water is less rigid than on the grouse moors because it is a much more solitary sport. If the sportsman is accompanied by a gillie it is considered bad form not to take his advice, as he surely knows more about the art of hooking fish than you. It is in poor taste to call him 'gillie', he should be known by either his Christian or surname and it is most selfish not to offer him a dram from your hip flask.

DO

wear green waders and dull clothes although it is said fish are colour-blind

tickle fish

tie your own flys

take the advice of the gillie or you will go away empty handed

learn to cast where you want to

boast about the one which got away – everybody else does

DON'T

wear a tweed hat with flies stuck all over it, but some form of headwear protects one against the unpleasant experience of hooking oneself

spin for salmon

describe fishing as angling – because that's what others do beside filled-in gravel pits

fish in someone else's water

cast to foul hook – this means dragging your hook across the stream in an attempt to hook the dorsal fin of a salmon – even though the fish fights better this way

Rivers to head for

IN	OUT
Grimesta (seven miles of the most exclusive fishing in the Outer Hebrides)	Tay (expensive but not very smart)
Tweed	Thames (supporting life once again but not ready for serious fishing)
Spey	
Oykell	Wharfe, West Yorkshire
Eden, Cumberland	Itchen
Usk	Test (a stockbrokers' river)
Avon (the top half above Salisbury)	
Nadder	
Park (only in the early part of the season)	
Brora, Sutherland	
Dee	

Hunting

Once it was social death to admit a loathing of the horse and total ignorance of all things equine but this is no longer the case. Yet still good horsemanship is admired – as is bravery on the hunting field and the polo field. The pursuit of 'the inedible' has always attracted a particular sort of person who, depending on your stance, you may believe to be indescribable or commendable. The upper class have never really liked foxes and regard them as vermin, considering that the best way of eliminating them from the countryside is by hunting. It is an issue which deeply divides the classes because it is held up as a barbaric amusement for the upper classes but actually some of its greatest patrons come from the yeomanry – small farmers, landowners and the like. Is it the Anglo-Saxon identification with animals which brings out the protesters with their aniseed sprays, or plain old-fashioned envy which motivates them to shout abuse at the ample women and blimpish men who assemble at every hunt meet?

Hunting retains its tradition and is a mystery to most people who have never roared through the countryside shouting 'Yorrocks!' or whatever. The frequency of a kill is limited but most hunting folk say that is not important – much more that they can go charging about leaping over blind ditches and fences and putting their bravado on show. A year hardly goes by without some member of the aristocracy taking a serious tumble, although hunting deaths seem to be less numerous than of old.

A hunt in full cry is an undeniably pretty sight but, for those who doubt their courage, beagling is a better way of ensuring that you will get home in one piece.

DO

ride side-saddle if you want to have real style – but be careful on the steeper jumps

open gates for the women and close them afterwards

offer around your stirrup-cup but don't drink too much – it will give you Dutch courage and end in a topple

be turned out correctly – no brown boots, for instance

ask permission to be excused if you only want a morning's hunting

remember the fox has *gone to ground* in an *earth*

remember the huntsmen wear *pinks* – not red

DON'T

refer to the pack as dogs, because they are *hounds*

ask for the fox's tail – it has a *brush*

gallop off in front of the master, who when he catches up with you will demand an explanation, and send you home if you continue to lead the field

carry your whip in a loop, as that is considered bad form

wear jewellery

ride across seed fields

express disgust when they 'blood' you at your first kill – it is tradition and the idea is to kill the fox;

The upper classes hate foxes

not be too worried about using bad language, as both sexes are prone to utter expletives

if you don't like it, give up hunting

hit out at protesters – as such behaviour confirms in their minds what despicable people hunt

Hunts

IN	OUT
Quorn	Eridge
Pytchley	South Pool Harriers
Bicester	Cottesmore
Beaufort	Portman
VWH (Vale of White Horse)	Bedale
Whaddon Chase	Almost any Home
Middleton	Counties pack
South Devon Hounds	
Fitzwilliam	
Heythrop	
Almost any Irish pack	

Yachts and things nautical
Yacht clubs

IN	OUT
Royal Yacht Squadron	Island Sailing Club
Royal Bombay Yacht Club	(Cowes)
Royal Ocean Racing Club	Royal Thames
Royal Corinthian	Cowes Corinthian

Clothes

IN	OUT
Docksiders	Stiletto heels
Topsiders	Open-toed sandals
Javelin boots (not yellow)	Clark's 'Docksider' type
Arran sweaters	shoes
Henri Lloyd jackets	M.&S. Guernseys

| Helli Hensen oilskins | All blazers with silver buttons (used to denote deck-staff in the old days) |

People

IN	OUT
Bob Fisher	Huey Long (of Ondine)
Peter Nicholson	Tony Boyden
Arthur Slater	Ted Heath (has a poor reputation for standing his round at Cowes)
Chris Dunning	Robin Aisher
Owen Aisher	Ted Turner
	Alan Bond

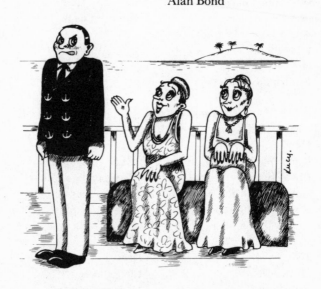

'Martini, please — you are staff?'

Races to enter

Fastnet (despite last year's disaster)
Sydney/Hobart
Cowes/Torquay powerboat
Dinard
Round the Island
Admiral's Cup

Harbours

IN	OUT
Hamble	Monaco
Dartmouth	Brighton
Chichester	St Catherine's Dock
St Malo	Poole
Western Scotland	Calais
Minorca	Mallorca

DO	DON'T
dip your ensign when passing Royalty or a Royal Navy ship	believe in the 'steam gives way to sail' code – no modern oil tanker can stop for you these days
abide by the rules of racing – or be considered an amateur	have fenders over the side while under way – considered very bad form
fly a Red Ensign (for all); fly a Blue Ensign (if you belong to a Royal Yacht Club which has a warrant), fly a White Ensign (only if you are Royalty, a RN ship, and members of the Royal Yacht Squadron) – but fly nothing if you are racing and then other craft will avoid you	leave your sick for others to clear up
	shoot at albatrosses
	insist on bringing tonic along for the gin – if you are racing it weighs too much; but pink gin is now considered OUT
	hoist a gin pennant – a flag which indicates drinks

not expect sympathy if you get cold because you have turned up in thin clothing – shivering women are despised

are available on board; monogrammed pennants are considered v. OUT

sail across the starting line if you are not entered in the race

Boats

IN	OUT
Cigarette power boats	Chris Craft – and all gin palaces
Cougar boats (James Beard)	Flying Fifteens
Solings	All wind surfers (for macho-men who wish to emulate Old Spice adverts)
Mirror dinghys	Canal barges
Thames barges	Thames houseboats
Nicholsons	
Riva	

Skiing

The invention of winter sports happened when members of the English aristocracy abandoned their grouse moors and took up residence in Switzerland. It is a well-known fact that when such groups of upper-class chaps gathered together they quickly became bored and so began to invent ways of making the time pass. In the same way as golf, football, cricket, squash and tennis (although the French have some claim upon the latter) were born, this desultory group of people just about invented winter sports.

Naturally this same group of people, who might have been mildly competitive towards each other, could never have foreseen the brouhaha that is every winter season on the Alpine pistes.

128

Like all our best ideas (the hovercraft, the television, the microchip), foreigners have come along and taken it to the logical conclusion – with the end result that the Brits have been excluded. The reason for this is twofold: the white stuff which falls in the Scottish highlands is not really snow but has the texture of tapioca pudding and is not conducive to making Ingmar Stenmarks of those who brave it; and the British nature is too amateur at heart to make any real impression upon continental skiers who have lived with the stuff since childhood.

All this has the sad consequence of making the average British skier look incredibly foolish to our European neighbours who have enabled the slopes to be opened up to the masses.

But the common herd can be avoided if the seeker after exclusivity is willing to pay for it. It is almost possible to judge how exclusive a resort is by the amount charged for a humble cup of coffee. You know you have made it when after being presented with the tab at say the Palace Hotel, Gstaad, for a cup or two you pay up with good grace without flinching. That is style – and you need a lot of style up there in the mountains. In Gstaad, which is *the après-ski* resort, you will be mingling with the Burtons (Richard and Suzie, Elizabeth and her Senator), the Sellers and the Sachs, and you must pass among them as if you belong.

It is as important to know the IN resorts, ski travel companies (the bad ones will send you to quite the wrong place), and the correct jargon if you wish to climb on the pistes. Of course it is not essential to actually ski but it is necessary to pretend that you have come all this way to get some in.

The upstart is easily spotted if he dons a brand-new ski suit hurriedly purchased in Lillywhites. It is sensible to break the thing in while back at home. Equally, hired

The upstart is easily spotted . . . in a new ski suit

boots and skis bearing the label of the local sports shop are a give-away. Bring your own.

While there is nothing wrong in wearing very smart equipment, the ski-nob, who probably learnt at a young age, does not feel the slightest shame in pulling on his plus-fours, jeans even or Guernsey sweater. It is quite chic to produce a pair of planks which go back to before the war. They may be quite useless to ski on but everyone will notice them and it will register that you are no newcomer to the slopes. Female ski-nobs, who have usually received a Swiss finishing-school education and even taken chalet work in order to subsidize skiing, are more accomplished than the men. The trouble is they tend to take the whole thing far too seriously and as a rule have rather large bottoms.

It is best to stay with friends in their chalets in the following resorts:

IN	OUT
Gstaad	St Moritz (southern end)
Verbier	Sauze D'Oux
Klosters	Davos
Meribel	Courcheval
Val d'Isere	Zermatt
Puy St Vincent	Tignes (Val Claret)
Lech	St Anton
Cervinia	Courmayeur
Morzine	Avoriaz
Wengen	Isola 2000
Les Gets	La Plagne
Les Arcs	Garmisch
Bugaboos	Innsbruck
Aspen, Colorado	Lake Placid, NY State
Kitzbuhl	Dolomites
	Andorra

Granada
Cortina
NSW, Australia

Travel companies

IN	OUT
Supertravel	Schools Abroad
John Morgan	Snowtime
Ski Snowball	Bladon Lines
Club Mediterranée	Mark Warner
	Ingams
	Flards
	Small World
	Blue Sky
	Erna Low
	Swans
	Global
	Thomson
	Cosmos
	Horizon
	Neilson

Ski equipment

IN	OUT
Pré	Hexcel
Olin	Kastle
Elan	Head
Atomic	Maxel
Dynastar	Rossignol
	Roy 'Hot Dogs'
	All compacts
	K2
	Fischer
	The Ski

Boots

IN	OUT
Dynafit	Garmont
Lange	Nordica
Koflach	Caber (very OUT)
Kronos	San Marco
Salomon SX90 (Equipe model only)	Hanson
Wellingtons	Scott
Royal Hunters	Nearly all 'Wop' boots

Clothing

IN	OUT
Anzi Besson	Japanese
Hec	Head
Daniel Hector	McGregor
Powderhorn	Fila
	All German clothing
	Head bands, gaiters
	Bum bags

Shops

IN	OUT
Alpine Sports	Pindisports
Harrods	Lillywhites
Sun and Snow	Moss Bros
Provincial ski shops	YHA

Ski bindings

IN	OUT
Tyrolia	Look
Solomon S727	All other Solomons
	Spademans
	Hope

Variations

IN	OUT	
Ski-jumping	Cross-country	depending on which country you're in
Hot-dogging (freestyle)	Langlauf	
Shussing	*Ski de fond*	
Stabbing foreigners with ski sticks	(all too much like hard work)	
Space Invaders	Gluwein/*Vin chaud*	
Citron pressé with Vodka	People who talk about black runs	
Black runs	High-altitude lip cream	
Helicopter skiing (including private planes)	Leather skins	
Asprey's hip flasks with Irish malt whiskey for sustenance	Ski conversation after seven p.m.	
Ski conversations to seven p.m.	Teetotallers and hot-chocolate drinkers	
	Artificial ski slopes	

16

Clubs

IN

Annabel's: Dark enough for indiscretion and owner Mark Birley claims to ban gossip columnists. Prince Charles makes the odd appearance, but don't count on seeing him. Rather too many pinstriped businessmen staying over with their 'personal assistants'.

Tramp: John Gold keeps out too many no-nos but allows in 'guests' who look as though they will not flinch at the price of a bottle of Krug. Still frequented by visiting film stars, footballers, singers and the late-sixties set.

Wedgie's: Greeter Dai Llewellyn has brought some glamour back to this King's Road club but the Deb of the Year contest is really for the end of Blackpool Pier – not a

OUT

The Garden: Now that the owner has parted with Regine, who gave her name to the club – its future is uncertain. Probably the prettiest club in London with real wild-fowl swimming on the stream. Mr Ram, the charming Indian proprietor, needs to attract new members of quality for it to take off. Prices could come down as an incentive.

Heaven: Has one of the best light shows of any club. But its emphasis is so heavily 'gay' that it cannot be considered IN.

Bennett: Battersea watering hole for people who live South of the River and like to boast about dancing above piranah fish and over the Roddy Llewellyn garden.

night club. Drink free if friends of the owner or the greeter.

Maunkberry's: Up the road from the smarter Tramp – but this spot has its own particular clientele. Very much the sleazy atmosphere of a speakeasy with laid-back rock musicians, starlets and *poseurs* sipping rum-and-cokes.

Legends: Can be entered on payment of a fee. Ex-punk – so pretty (extraordinary) people are not ashamed of what they do on the dance floor. For the younger set.

Blitz: Covent Garden wine bar by day and punk disco by night. Only for the *cognoscenti* – or arch *poseurs*.

Hell: Although gay in flavour it does not make the uninitiated feel uncomfortable.

Raffles: It is reputed that Prince Charles once visited this club, which resembles a library; has an unhappy habit of shutting its doors at around two a.m. to avoid drunken guests.

Dial 9: Pretty but not a first-division bopperaria.

J. Arthur's: Hardly smart.

The Alley: Not the IN place.

'When I go to a restaurant or a discotheque I like to think that I'm largely anonymous.'

Nigel Dempster (ex-diary writer)

Gentlemen's

IN	OUT
White's (the one they all want to join)	Royal Automobile (who have opened up membership to shopkeepers, etc.)
Turf	
Pratt's	
Buck's	Brook's
Beefsteak	Athenaeum
Boodle's	Savile
Cavalry and Guards	Garrick
Puffin's (Edinburgh)	Eccentric
	Travellers
	Oriental
	East India, Sports, Public School and Devonshire
	Oxford and Cambridge
	Reform
	Carlton
	The American
	Bath

17

Knowledge

Champagne

IN	OUT
Lanson Red Label	Lanson Black Label
Bollinger, Special Cuvée	Charles Heidsieck
Salon	Mumm
Tattinger Comtes de	Veuve Clicquot
Champagne	Mercier, Private Brut
Louis Roederer Crystal	M&C Dom Perignon
Moet & Chandon, Dry	Perrier Jouet
Imperial	Ayala
Philipponnat	
Pol Roger	
Pommery and Greno	
Krug	

Drinks

IN	OUT
Bloody Mary	Rum and coke
Daiquiri (frozen)	Brandy Alexander
Dry Martini	Wine Cup
Chilled port	Gin and orange
Whiskey sour	Whisky Mac
Harvey Wallbanger	Rum nogg
Gin and tonic	Snowball (whatever it is)
Pink gin	Tia Maria
Cognac	Tequila Sunrise
All *eau de vie* (Kirsch, etc.)	Dubonnet
Calvados	Scrumpy
Armagnac	Campari and tonic
Single malt whisky	Bacardi

Sloe gin
Buck's fizz
Crème de menthe frappé
Screwdriver
Sake (with Japanese food)
Tom Collins
Sherry
Cointreau
Drambuie
Le Grand Marnier
Kir
Pimms No. 1 and No. 6
   (to order)
Kummel
Madeira

Gin fizz
Crème de cacao
Raki
Retsina
Rye and dry
Lager and lime
Sangria
Real ale
Irish Mist
Benedictine
Port and lemon
Vin de table
Chartreuse
Black Velvet

Chocolates

IN
Harrods full strength liqueur
La Toque Blanche
Cadbury's Nuts
Bendicks Sporting and
   Military
Bendicks Superfine
   Handmade
Suchard Elegance
Lindt
Leonidas (with fresh cream
   and butter from Belgium –
   at Harrods)
Royal Assortment, Droste
Baci
Clare of London
Godiva of Belgium

OUT
Black Magic
After Eight
Quality Street
Galaxy
Dairy Box by Rowntree
Devon Milk
Moonlight
Terry's All Gold
Mackintosh's Week-End

Scent

IN	OUT
Joy	Eau de Fleurs by Nina Ricci
Arpège by Lanvin	Dioressence
Chloe by Lagerfeld	Miss Worth
Cabochard by Gres	Jontue by Revlon
Cardin by Pierre Cardin	Charlie by Revlon
Lauren by Ralph Lauren	5 a.m. by Yardley
Chanel No. 19	Chique
Opium by Yves St Laurent	Chanel No. 5
Nahema by Guerlain	Fidgi by Guy Laroche
Givenchy 111	Blue Grass by Elizabeth Arden
Oscar de la Renta	L'Air du Temps by Nina Ricci
Metal by Paco Rabanne	Elle *parfum de toilette*
Eau de Patou by Jean Petou	Chantilly by Houbigant
Cavale	L'Aimant by Coty
	Blasé
	Vu by Ted Lapidus
	Femme by Rochas

Emporiums

IN	OUT
Fortnum and Mason	Barkers
Harrods (the food hall is a religious experience to behold)	Whiteleys
	Dickins and Jones
	John Lewis
Liberty & Co.	Scotch House
Harvey Nichols	Conran
Simpsons	Habitat
Fenwicks	Mothercare
Marks & Spencer (for knickers)	Bentalls
	Jaeger

General Trading Company
Aquascutum
Chic of Hampstead
Browns
Piero de Monzi
Fiorucci
Peter Jones
Hamleys
Lillywhites
Balloon (for maternity stuff)
Jack Barclay
Janet Reger
Place Vendôme
Burberrys
Bombacha
Claude Montana
Loewe
Christian Dior
Philip Antrobus
Chaumet
Cartier
Hermes
Asprey
David Morris
Watches of Switzerland
Floris
Galleria – Monte Carlo (for the plush flush)
Paxton and Whitfields (just smell it)
Charles de Temple
M. Gerard
Tiger, Tiger
New Man

Swan and Edgar
Mappin and Webb
Arding and Hobbs
Tessier
Gucci
Reject China Shop
Selfridges
Debenhams
Garrards
Chiesmans
Woolworths

Health farms

'Ever since she had the children, Jan's got fatter and fatter. She's nearly thirteen stone now – which is a big worry for someone who used to be a model. To give you an example – I'm looking at the Caribbean and Jan's in front. I can see Jan but I can't see the sea.'

Gavin Hodge, crimper, speaking about his wife Jan Burdett

Society demands prettiness from its members, who being aware of the way they look will take care to present a clean and healthy look which spells success. The three-day growth which became popular in the late seventies after pop-stars like Paul McCartney and David Essex went to parties without bothering to shave has given way to a less debauched style. The ravages which a surfeit of wine, late nights and other indulgences can produce in the active socializer may force him to take stock and review his health. The sedentary clubber is most at risk and before long his contemporaries will remark upon his wan complexion and expanding waistline. A trip to the health farm is the answer where, contrary to popular belief, much fun can be had – so long as all your strength has not drained away with the diet of lettuce, carrot juice and lemon tea.

A ten-day trip will cost somewhere in the region of £250 – after which you will be returned to the fold minus your beer gut (OUT) with shiny eyes and sun-bed tan, fit to tackle another six months of candle-burning at both ends.

IN	OUT
Forest Mere	Stobo Castle, Scotland
Grayshott	Henlow Grange
Inglewood	Ragdale
Champneys	Enton Hall
	Tyringham
	Shrublands

TV programmes

IN	OUT
Coronation Street (for actors)	Songs of Praise
	Starsky and Hutch
Credo	The Waltons
The Book Programme	Dallas
Most BBC documentaries	Match of the Day
All Alan Whicker travelogues	It's a Knockout
	That's Life
Panorama	Agony
Not the Nine O'Clock News	Open University
The Muppets	Newsnight
Blue Peter	Crossroads
Jim'll Fix It	Angels
To the Manor Born	Grange Hill
Question Time (R. Day)	News at Ten (since Reggie went)
One Man and His Dog	
Dr Who	Emmerdale Farm
Barbara Woodhouse on Dogs	Hawaii Five-O
	International Darts
Tales of the Unexpected	Police 5 with Shaw Taylor
Bless Me, Father	Sale of the Century
University Challenge	Streets of San Francisco
The South Bank Show	Winner Takes All
All Creatures Great and Small	The Sky at Night
	The Benny Hill Show
What the Papers Say	
World in Action	
Worzel Gummidge	

Cars

IN	OUT
TR7 Drophead	Rolls-Royce Camargue
Lotus Esprit	Allegro
Porsche 924 Turbo	Toyota Starlet
Alfasud Super 1.3	Skoda

Rover 3500 V8S
Range-Rover (for country use)
Audi Quattro
Matra Bagheera
Lancia Stratos
AC 3000ME (for the speed king)
Aston Martin Volante
Mini
Renault 5
BMWs (all)
Bristol 412S.2
Citroën 2CV (for the eccentric)
Ferrari (all)
De Tomaso Pantera GTS
Fiat X1/9
Fiat Strada
Jeep Cherokee Chief (v. IN)
Maserati Khamsin
Mercedes-Benz 450SL
Morgan Plus 8
Open Monza
Reliant Scimitar GTE
TVR Tasmin
Volkswagen Golf Convertible
Bentley (any pre-1968)
Austin Morris 1000
Triumph Dolomite Sprint
Mallalieu (hand-built thirties tourers)
Alvis
Cougar

Volvo (the car of the bourgeois with its non-extinguishable lights)
Lada
Jaguars (new and used)
All Japanese cars (no style)
Mini Scamp
Audi Avanti
Morris Marina (unless office car)
Caterham Super Seven
Daihatsu F20 (Jeep imitation)
Citroën CX Athena
Crayford Cortina
Fiat 126 (butler's runabout)
Ford Escort
Ford Granada
Ford Mustang Ghia Turbo
Pantha Lima (too showy)
MGB GT (Young Conservatives' car)
Peugeot 504
Talbot Sunbeam T1
Matra Rancho
Volvo 343
Daf
Daimler (Jag in all but name)
Hillman Imp
Lamborghini Espada (*nouveau*'s car)
Moskvich
Simca

Which helicopter?

IN	OUT
Hughes 500 D (a mere £145,500)	Alouette
	Dauphin
Bell 206 Jet Ranger 3	Puma
Enstrom Shark (cheap at £60,000)	Wessex (too military)
Bolkow 105 (for aerobatics)	Bell 222 (eight-passenger craft costing £575,000)
Agusta 109	Aerospatiale Squirrel
Sikorsky Spirit	
Long Ranger	

Charters

IN	OUT
B-Cal	Bristow
Alan Mann	British Airways
Sloane Aviation	
Air Hanson	
McAlpine	
Gleneagle	

Which plane?

IN	OUT
HS 125	Lear Jet
Piper Navajo C	Beechcraft Super King Air 200
Cessna 340 A	Piper Aztec
Pitt Special (for loop-the-loopers)	Beech Baron
Boeing 737	Corvette
Pilatus Porter	Boeing 707
Jetstar	Seneca 2
	De Havilland Canada DHC-6 Twin Otter

Airlines

IN	OUT
Air Jamaica	Turkish
Varig	Kuwait Airways
Qantas	Kenya Airways
Olympic	Nigeria Airways
British	Zambia Airways
Swissair	Dan Air
Singapore	Syriaair
Air India	Ethiopian
Air Lanka	Aeroflot
KLM	Iran Air
Austrian	Iraqi Airways
Pakistan	Libyan Arab
Pan Am	Royal Brunei
Laker	Viasa Airways
UTA	Aer Lingus
Caledonian	Air Målta
TWA	El Al
Air France	Iberia Air Lines
Sabena	Tunis Air
Air Canada	Lan Chile
Alitalia	Yugoslav
Japan	Sudan Airways
Lufthansa	South African Airways
Finnair	Air Malawi
	Air Zaire

Smokes

IN	OUT
Gitanes Internationales	Winston
Gauloise	Marlboro
Fribourg and Treyer Number One	John Player Special
	Roll your own
Dunhill International	Kent
Sullivans No. 1 Turkish	Benson and Hedges

Lambert and Butler KS
Camel
Balkan Sobranie

St Moritz
Rothmans International
Guards
Woodbines
Everest
Cool
No. 6
555 State Express
Silk Cut
Senior Service
Pipes

It is most fashionable to smoke nothing at all.

Dogs – breeds

IN	OUT
Basset Hounds	Afghan Hounds
Beagles	Borzois
Bloodhounds	Whippets
Foxhounds (for hunting)	Irish Wolfhounds
English Setters	Greyhounds
Irish Setters	Airdale Terriers
Pointers	Cairn Terriers
Retrievers	Welsh Terriers
Red Setters	Alsatians
Spaniels (Springers)	Boston Terriers
Bull Terriers	Chow Chows
Sealyham Terriers	Collies
Staffordshire Bull Terriers	Dobermann Pinschers
Bulldogs	Poodles
Dalmatians	Schipperkes
Great Danes	Miniature Schnauzers
Newfoundlands	Welsh Corgis (Cardigan
Old English Sheepdogs	and Pembroke)
Pyrenean Mountain Dogs	Black and Tan Terriers
St Bernards	Griffons

Shih Tzus
King Charles Spaniels
Pomeranians
Pugs
Yorkshire Terriers
Jack Russells
Shar-Pei

Italian Greyhounds
Papillons
Pekingese
Otter Hounds
Labradors (Yellow)
Rhodesian Ridgebacks

Dogs – names

IN	OUT
Baron	Whisky
* Brush	Fido
Chipper	Rex
Piper	Bite
* Shadow	Fang
* Sparky	Kill
* Smoky	Nelson
* Jolly	Patch
* Myth	Puss
* Fable	Tramp
Pipkin	Taffy
* Socks	Pudding
Tivvy (in memory of a very fine if not a little neurotic Bobtail)	Siggy
	Daisy
	Jock
Sadie	Trigger
McMuck	Tu-tu
Rinka	Pooch
Emma	Florence
Lucy	Penny
Melody	Lucky
Music	Flash
Nero	Dart
Bull's Eye	Fred
Butcher	Spillane
Enoch	Kafka

Poo	Kipling
Bo	Kim
Smelly	Pook
George	Rover
Oscar	Honey
Archy	Coffee
Rupert	Ale
Nigel	
Claret	

Point of interest: * denotes Royal Corgis – but Chipper and Piper are the results of the amorous advances of Princess Margaret's dachshund Pipkin. History does not relate if this 'accident' was by design, but the Kennel Club would not approve.

Cats

IN	OUT
Blue Persians	Feral
Siamese	Manx
Abyssinians	Manul
Burmese	
Chinchilla	

Pets for the home

IN	OUT
Ducks	Foxes
Geese (good watchdogs)	Guinea-fowl
Doves	Pheasants (Golden)
Cavies (guinea pigs)	Ferrets
Golden hamsters	Goldfish (OK in lakes)
Wild boar (they can be	Toads/frogs
house-trained and are	Gerbils
intelligent – if they behave	Rats
they make good pets; if	Mice
they don't, eat them)	Terrapins

Falcons
Monkeys
Loris
Bush-babies
Ponies
Donkeys
Goats
Hedgehogs
Tortoises
Chickens (particularly
  bantams)
Tapir (if you have the space)

Insects, stick, etc.
Worms (earth and glow)
Snakes (all)
Caged birds, parrots, etc.
Racing pigeons
Rabbits
Lions
Iguana (impossible to
  house-train and low on
  affection)

Wild boar can be house-trained

Holidays
Summer

IN	OUT
Bolivia	Bahrain
Botswana	Congo
Brazil	Cyprus
China	Nigeria
Greek Island cruise	Bangladesh
Egypt	Hong Kong
Mauritius	Korea
Mexico	Costa del anything
Philippines	Morocco
Penang	Saudi Arabia
Ibiza	Seychelles
Salzburg (take in festival)	United Arab Emirates
Zambia	Venice (pongs this time of
Yorkshire Dales	year)
Scotland	Uganda
	Miami
	Lake District
	Ireland

Winter

IN	OUT
Gstaad	St Moritz
Seychelles	Canary Islands
Mustique	Pakistan
Fiji	Russia (cultural tour)
Sri Lanka	Hawaii
Bali	Oman
Tibet	Ghana
India (Himalayan	Ecuador
adventure)	Bahamas
Japan	New Zealand
Malaysia	Phukit Island
Papua, New Guinea	Falkland Islands

Australia – Great Barrier Reef	Aviemore, Scotland
Barbados	Jamaica
Cuba	
Kenya	

Estate agents

IN	OUT
Knight Frank and Rutley	Harrods Estates
Aylesford	De Groot Collis
Hamptons	Sturgis & Sons
Savills	Mellersh and Harding
Smith Gore	Marsh and Parsons
Cluttons	Gross, Fine and Kreiger
Humberts	Conrad Ritblat
John German, Ralph, Pay	Benham and Reeves
Chestertons	Glentree Estates
W. A. Ellis	Park Lord
Ridley & Co.	Debenham, Tewson and Chinnock
Tufnells	
T. Maskell	Charles Saunders
McKenzie Ide and Co.	Algulf Estates
Jackson-Stops & Staff	Gascoigne-Pees
George Trollope & Sons	Boyd & Boyd
Bernard Thorpe	Fox & Sons
Winkworth	Mann & Co.
Strutt and Parker	Messenger May Baverstock
	Lane Fox & Partners
	Druce & Co.

'Quite honestly, I hate living in a dirty house so much that if my cleaner is on holiday I have to go out and stay in an hotel.'

Ms Pat Booth

Fashionable causes and charities

IN	OUT
East African Flying Doctor Service	Actors' Benevolent Fund
British Heart Foundation	Entertainment Artistes' Benevolent Fund
Cancer Research Campaign	Musicians' Benevolent Fund
Council for Environmental Conservation	Officers' Families Fund
The Guide Dogs for the Blind Association	Anything to do with 'cleaning up TV' – Whitehouse-style
Order of St John	Homosexual Equality
Red Cross (v. county)	Legalize Cannabis Campaign
RNLI	Real Ale/Bread Campaigns
Save the Children	Stop All Racist Tours
The Corporation of the Sons of the Clergy	Action on Smoking and Health
Anything to do with Wales	CND (remember?)
Friends of the Earth	Freedom Organization for the Right to Enjoy Smoking Tobacco
NSPCC	The Lord's Day Observance Society
National Trust	RSPCA

Mind improvement, therapy and growth
(see Language – Psycobabble)

IN	OUT
Metamorphic Massage – prenatal foot therapy	Insight (safe and bourgeois, whose main public proponents are B. Levin and Arianna Stassinopoulos)
R. D. Laing (Scottish guru)	
Zone Therapy	
Shiatsu	

Alexander Technique
Psychosynthesis
Jungian thought
Gestalt Therapy (where
    value is placed on feeling
    and less on thinking)
Boyesen – near-Reichian,
    biodynamic psychology

Transactional analysis –
    was v. big in New York
    with everyone either
    playing the role of victim
    or persecutor
TM (old hat)
EST (one long ego bash
    which doesn't work)
Exegesis (Robert
    D'Aubigny is the man to
    watch)
Silva method of mind
    control

18

The Music Machine

'Our audiences are more computer-programmer types than hippies. Unlike in the sixties, it's more about how you feel inside today.'

Vince Ely, drummer with Psychedlic Furs

<table>
<tr><td colspan="2" align="center">Music papers</td></tr>
<tr><td>IN</td><td>OUT</td></tr>
<tr><td>Music Week (the business paper for those in the know)
New Musical Express</td><td>Sounds
Record Mirror (weenybopper paper trying to get heavy)
Melody Maker</td></tr>
</table>

<table>
<tr><td colspan="2" align="center">Groups</td></tr>
<tr><td>IN</td><td>OUT</td></tr>
<tr><td>Police (dyed-blond three piece who are a wow in the USA)
Thin Lizzy (the society-ligging Phil Lynott recently married comedian Leslie Crowther's daughter Caroline)
Genesis and Pink Floyd (a flavour of the sixties here, but still impressing a new generation of fans)</td><td>Blondie (Debbie Harry now turning drools to yawns)
Bob Dylan (the socially aware poet-singer who has now turned to God as old fans have turned to new heroes)
Boomtown Rats (sold out to society, so get them along to play at your dance. But Bob Geldof can't be forgiven for</td></tr>
</table>

The Who (particularly Pete Townsend; have kept very 'street' in appeal)

The Pretenders (watch them grow)

Lene Lovitch (weird part-American *chanteuse*)

Any Reggae bands

B. B. King or any old bluesman

making the stunning and rude Paula Yates his wife. Did you know she was once fired from a TV station for wearing smelly rubber trousers?)

Elvis Costello (bespectacled singing hero who is yesterday's flavour)

The Jam

David Essex

Record companies

IN	OUT
2 Tone (Coventry-based mini who have scored 10 hits with 10 releases)	Polydor
	RCA
Dindisc	United Artists
Stiff	EMI
Gun (a shot in the dark)	Ariola and Hansa
Any small record label	Island
Chrysalis	

Record producers

IN	OUT
Nick Lowe (new music man)	George Martin
Chris Thomas (ex-Sex Pistols person)	Ben Findon (Disco old-timer and mentor to the v. OUT Dooleys)
Hugh Murphy (trying hard to conceal the fact that he produced the surprise hit of the year, 'Captain Beaky', with Keith Michell)	David Essex (perhaps the only person who considers himself a producer)
	Mike Chapman

Mickie Most (millionaire
man about town,
TV-face and boss of
RAK records)

Follow these music styles	*But don't bother with these*
Reggae/Ska derivations	Disco (absolutely dead and
Heavy Metal	time the smarter clubs
Mod Music	started spinning new
Good cover-versions of	sounds)
oldies	Euro-pop
R and B	Ballads
Jazz	Bad cover-versions of old
All classics	songs
	Jazz fusion

Terminology

IN	OUT
Street	Punk
Hanging in there	Far Out
Head-bangers (state	Boppers/Bopping
induced by listening to	Getting it together
Heavy Metal)	Straights
Concept	Smoking
Turkeys (idiots)	Weird
Sniffing	
Off the wall	

Radio stations

Listen to these	*Don't bother about these*
Radio One	British Forces
Radio Four	Capital
Radio Three (for serious	Any local commercial
music)	Radio Luxembourg
Local Radio (BBC)	Radio Two (except at
	night)

Disc jockeys

IN	OUT
Kid Jensen	Tony Blackburn
John Peel	Jimmy Savile (a charity
Mike Read	worker)
Paul Gambaccini	Simon Bates
Anne Nightingale	All commercial station
Any good local spinners	spinners
	Tommy Vance
	Kenny Everett
	Adrian Love

Pop persons

IN	OUT
Marianne Faithful	Don Arden
Pauline McLeod (rock hack)	Tony Stratton-Smith
Howard Marks (No. 1	(horse-race loving boss
record promotion man)	of Charisma Records)
Chris Wright (party-giving	Jonathan King
head of Chrysalis)	Andrew Lloyd Webber and
Simon Draper	Tim Rice (quiz show
John Walters (John Peel's	personalities)
producer on Radio One)	John Lyndon (ex-Johnny
Tony Satchell (music	Rotten of Sex Pistols)
broker)	Larry Adler
	Bob Harris
	Tony Hatch

General

IN	OUT
Small companies	Multinational
Girl singers	corporations
Multiracial groups	Foreign groups
Those with street feel but	Groups with banks of
still into *gelt*	equipment

Fun publicity	Mogul-style rip-off
Live music	merchants
Films based around rock	Advertising hypes
(*The Rose*)	Plush 48-track recording
Cocaine and glue	studios
Black-and-white colour	Cannabis and heroin
patterns	
Experimental music of all	
kinds	

How IN are you?

Does your diary overflow with the names of the people who matter and whose sociability quotient is rated highly? If you can claim friendship with a member of Royalty score 20 socio-acceptable points, 18 for an archbishop, 15

'. . . 1 ex-king, 4 bishops and 2 gossip columnists, is that right, darling?'

for a duke, 8 for a marquess, 7 for a bishop, 5 for an earl, 4 for viscounts, barons, lesser titles and members of cabinet, 3 for judges, ex-kings, hostesses and hosts on the IN list, 2 for MPs, listed jet-setters, and members of the team on both IN and OUT sides; and one point for photographers, actors, models, millionaires, interior decorators, gossip columnists and club owners. If you can only claim an acquaintance score half-marks.

Anyone scoring over 200 points can count himself a courtier and a socialite of the highest esteem and such a person will never be short of an invitation. Those mustering 150 points will have an excellent knowledge of contemporary society and can claim genuine friendship with a number of people who matter. Someone scoring 100 points thinks he/she is better connected than they really are and is probably a social climber. Those who could honestly only award themselves 50 points need to read this book carefully and spend a few more nights around town. Anyone scoring less is probably a sculptor chiselling away in the middle of Romney Marsh, a monk in retreat, or someone with a terrible personal problem which their best friend has not told them about, or he is simply a country-loving yokel who does not give a fig (or a firkin?) what people get up to down there in the smoke.